The Transformational Imperative

The Transformational Imperative

PLANETARY REDEMPTION THROUGH
SELF-REALIZATION

SHUNYAMURTI

Cover Design by Narayan (Ryan Brennan)

Layout Design by Sat Yoga Institute
Tel: (506) 2288-3294 / 8891-6486
Email: info@satyogainstitute.org
URL: www.satyogainstitute.org
San José, Costa Rica

ISBN-10: 0-615-22139-4
ISBN-13: 978-0-615-22139-7

Published by Sat Yoga Publications, Doral, Florida
In cooperation with BookSurge Publishing, Charleston, South
Carolina

Printed in the United States of America by BookSurge Publishing

Visit www.amazon.com and www.booksurge.com
to order additional copies.

Contents

Foreword

The essays you are about to read were sent originally to students of the spiritual path of Sat Yoga in various parts of the world. The purpose of these writings was, and is, to support and encourage serious spiritual warriors at all phases of the inner struggle to achieve the imperative next leap of human evolution—what the ancient spiritual tradition of Sat Yoga refers to as the Supreme Liberation.

This goal is no mere utopian diversion for new-age dilettantes, but a scientifically defensible, ethically imperative, and psychologically requisite attainment if we are going to meet the mounting challenges to human survival. The general level of our psychological development is insufficient to withstand the stresses of cultural collapse, let alone those of the coming ecological failure and cataclysmic geophysical shifts. The apocalyptic clouds of global war, pandemics, famine, and social breakdown are darkening and advancing every day. Only a radical transformation of human consciousness, in which critical numbers of us mobilize the full range of our psycho-spiritual potentials—our creative intelligence, healing powers, telepathic communication, and empathic peacemaking capacities, among others—and organize new centers of higher culture to fill the vacuum and provide leadership when the current system has fallen of its own dead weight, will enable us to bring about a renaissance on our sacred Earth.

The goal of Sat Yoga is transcendence of the ego. The ego can be defined as the normal-neurotic state that most of us are in, which involves the belief that the self is the body/mind, with

existence that is temporary and separate from others and from the universe as a whole. Technically, the ego is a complex three-tiered structure. In addition to the conscious mind, there is an unconscious sector with multiple layers of repressed psychic sediment. In addition, there is a censoring apparatus responsible for the homeostatic maintenance of the ego with its customary defense mechanisms. These defenses are responsible for most of the ego's pathological behavior patterns. Beyond the ego lies the trans-rational Self, which Yogis call the Atman. This real Self is one with the universe as a whole, and is serene, loving, peaceful, and wise. Realization of the Atman brings about a radical transformation of one's life.

For a fortunate few, the effort to transcend ego-consciousness is swift and sweet. Upon learning that the ego is illusory, consciousness drops identification with body and personality and enters the state of pure blissful awareness. Then the gift of the use of higher powers in the service of humanity unfolds easily with further training. For most of us, however, the struggle to transcend ego is long and arduous, requiring the rigorous working-through of tenacious unconscious fixations and primitive defenses. These essays are designed to be of use to those at all stages of the journey, at all points on the spectrum of psycho-spiritual development.

This text is not intended to substitute for intensive one-to-one work with an adept spiritual guide, who is trained to function as a catalyst to accelerate the psycho-spiritual development of others, including the purification of the unconscious mind and the emergence of *siddhis* (higher Yogic powers of awakened mind). Working alone is far more difficult. The ego has many ways to deceive and divert one from the central task. Defense mechanisms built into the unconscious ego structure can too easily maintain submerged fragments of narcissistic consciousness in the fog of Maya (illusion) while convincing you that you are achieving illumination. A skillful, truthful, dispassionate guide and a supportive spiritual community that can recognize blind spots and

that do not collude with imaginary versions of enlightenment are essential allies on the difficult ascent of the holy mountain within.

Sat Yoga is a path that integrates the teachings of the ancient Yogic sages with all the esoteric traditions of both East and West, fleshed out with the aid of conceptual tools gleaned from the most recent forms of depth psychology and psychoanalysis, phenomenology, and other human sciences ranging from semiotics and linguistics to sociology and anthropology. In addition, this path makes use of the findings of mathematics (especially set theory, topology, and higher-dimensional geometries) and the hard sciences, from quantum physics to biology and chemistry.

The insights from these disciplines can offer crucial analogies and metaphors to aid in the understanding of the relationship between the complexity of ego-consciousness and the simple nature of higher awareness that can help center the mind in a state of alert stillness, in preparation for the attainment of final liberation.

Sat Yoga is an integrative path, one function of which is to demonstrate that all religions are pointing to the same immanent/transcendent truth. It is a truth that we must come to embody—if we are to meet the challenges of the unprecedented crisis that is upon us.

It is no exaggeration to call this the decisive moment in human history. It is not just the end of one era and the beginning of another. It represents the end of a cycle of natural existence for the whole planetary biosphere, and is resulting in the extinction of nearly all the higher life forms on Earth. The survival of humanity itself is in question. At this unique evolutionary moment, the energies of consciousness, our Supreme Being, are more active. They can be more easily and palpably felt with less effort than at other times, at least by those who ask with faith and love for understanding and assistance in bringing this process to the most fruitful culmination.

The inspiration, serenity, and empowerment accessible as a result of ego transcendence and union with our immanent/transcendent Supreme Self are the necessary attainments to complete the quantum leap required of humanity. We are called upon now to grow up as a species, to face reality, to renounce our narcissism, our mendacity, our addictions to power and pleasure, and our intentional ignorance and denial. To accomplish all that, we must find our real center, known in Yoga as *Atman*.

The act of profound centering, or meditation, has a long history as the core practice of Yoga and the later spiritual traditions based on Yoga. Meditation involves the silencing of the mind. In inner silence, ego transcendence leads into contemplation and finally numinous realization of the transfinite Real. The power, insight, and sublime presence of the Absolute can then work through the individual body/mind. This produces *Avatara*, ego death and spiritual rebirth: the aim and object of all true religion.

As more and more individuals undergo this sacred metamorphosis, the effect on human consciousness of this higher vibratory frequency will shift humanity as a whole into a new level of coherence, producing morphogenetic effects throughout the chain of Being. This change in turn will hasten the end of the current *yuga*, or human evolutionary era, and the birth of the next. We are at the brink of the end of the world as we know it, the climax of the age of Kali Yuga, the age of conflict, brutality and vice, in which humans have fallen to the lowest moral and spiritual level possible—and potentially at the beginning of the new age that every religion has longed for as Paradise, the Kingdom of Heaven on Earth, or Sat Yuga, the golden age of the manifestation of our highest possibilities for truth, virtue, harmony, happiness, creativity, and unity. This is no mere myth. We have the power to make it a living reality. Some of us now alive may in fact survive to see the transition take place in our current lifetimes.

It is hoped that the following essays will be of help in preparing for this momentous planetary transfiguration. Once the pieces of the puzzle fall into place, we can recognize that what, on the surface, seem to be tragic phenomena—such as global warming, biological plagues, economic meltdowns, world wars and general social collapse—are really blessings in disguise. All the above are the birth pangs of a new world. Of course, it could yet die in childbirth. We must take every precaution to protect it. Humans are being put under pressures never before known. Some will crack under these pressures. Others will transform. If we create communities that are mutually supportive in fulfilling our transformational imperative, we are more likely to achieve a successful renaissance. The metamorphosis of humans into what have in mythic discourse been called angels and gods can only occur under such extreme circumstances as we are facing, but we must respond adequately.

We have already entered the long-awaited season of the spawning of a new generation of divine beings. It happens only once in numerous millennia. We are fortunate to be present at this most wonderful (super)natural event. Not even the hatching of sea turtles or the birthing of whale calves can compare. It is even more wonderful when we realize that we have been chosen to participate. And we have. Some have already recognized that the divine transformative process is underway. And in a very few, it is already complete.

Nature is about to give birth to Supernature, to the crown of Creation. The seed of Supernature is within us all. If we cultivate the Godseed, through devoted meditation, egoless action, communal synergy, and constant compassionate mindfulness, the shell of the ego will soon crack and the Supreme Self will be revealed and released to act through yet another being. Global destruction and planetary renewal will both occur simultaneously. It is important to identify not with what is dying, but with what is being born.

The following essays are intended to help you orient yourself to the changes that are already happening within you, as well as

11

without. Please share this information with others who are also sensing the portentous coming of the new dawn. Those who feel helpless to do anything to stop the onrushing suicidal death drive of our present societies need to know that there is nothing to fear. Our terminally ill culture of oppression is being taken out of its misery once and for all. Environmentalists worried about the mass extinction of species should also be not afraid. The power of Nature to create new life is limitless.

It is imperative is that we transform ourselves so that we deserve to live in a world restored to its full health and beauty, so that the laws of karma shift into gear on our behalf. The accumulation of merit, as Buddha said, will be decisive. We must merit salvation. Only through the purification of our souls and our total dedication to God, through our love for this world and for all beings, who in fact are God in deep disguise, can we achieve the fulfillment of our own potential: our transmutation into divine beings. This is the one mandate communicated by God through all the prophets of all religions. Now is the moment to fulfill the transformational imperative.

Know that you are not alone. Many of us are working together, on both subtle and gross levels of reality. And the Supreme One is secretly guiding us all. The whole truth shall soon be revealed. In the meantime, remember God with love at every moment. That is the one quintessential key to salvation.

Namaste,
Shunyamurti

PROLOGUE
The Search

The Search

The soul is like a salmon. It seeks to return to the place of its birth.

For the salmon, that means leaving its comfortable known habitat in the deep ocean, swimming to the mouth of a strange river, one that it has seen only once in its life, and beginning a long haul upstream. Soon it will be struggling fiercely against the current, finally having to leap cascading waterfalls, then to wriggle through shallows and under logs, before it reaches its destination. And on the way, the salmon must face the greatest obstacles of every sort, from the predations, contaminations, dams, and debris of humans, to hungry bears and other beasts, the resistance of Nature itself, to arrive at last at the place of its spawning.

Most will not make it. But among the few who do, there is no question of having arrived at the right place. Somehow, it knows, it remembers the very spot of its own origin. And there it mates, with another of the same brood but complementary gender. One lays the eggs, the other fertilizes them, and then both will die, having fully completed their life cycle.

How is the soul like a salmon? We, too, at some moment in life, realize the uncanny need to return to our transcendent point of origin. Societies have historically accommodated that need by establishing pilgrimage destinations and routes, physical journeys to the source of some sacred river or holy land or numinous object that represents our Supreme Being. But the real pilgrimage is within. And we know intuitively, when that moment comes, that we must enter into our inmost consciousness to re-find our original essence.

In contemporary society, there is no recognition of this ultimate drive of the soul. And so the inner pilgrimage is too often short-circuited, or else co-opted by social institutions into a more limited intention. But the soul, like the salmon, will not settle for a false destination. It must return to its true point of origin. Whether this point is called the Self, God, Allah, Buddha nature, Shiva, or Brahman, is unimportant. The point of origin is beyond names and beliefs. It lies in another dimension that is both beyond the world and yet here and now, more intimately here than our own ego-consciousness. To get here requires only the realization that we have not truly been here and now, that ego-consciousness is out of touch with its inmost Self, that the world of our ego-consciousness is an artificial construct of language that veils the Real. The journey begins when we allow that construct to drop away.

The inner journey for us is as perilous as the heroic effort to leap upstream to the source-point is for the salmon. We must leave behind the comfort of the ego's habitus, the defenses and behavior patterns that enable us to maintain the illusion of a unified personal self, and face the psychic fractures, phantasies, conflicts, and currents of repressed affect from which we have hidden for so many years. To face the fact that our real Being is unknown to our own consciousness requires great courage. Yet the soul unerringly knows, even though the ego does not remember, where it is going and what it is seeking.

The soul encompasses the ego. Ego is the personal, three-tiered, structure of hardened mind-energy that constantly emits routine thoughts to maintain the homeostasis of its identity construct through time. It consists of a conscious level of subjectivity, and an unconscious cache of repressed thoughts, memory traces, axioms, phantasies, and other identificatory fixations. Between the conscious and the unconscious levels dwells the ego's central intelligence agency, that is responsible for maintaining defense mechanisms; enactment of drives in accordance with phantasy scenarios; superego judgments to maintain control over the conscious mind; constant deception of the conscious mind as to its true agenda; and the general direction of behavior, according to that hidden agenda.

But unbeknownst to the ego, the encompassing power of the soul leads one's life in directions that differ from the desires of the ego. The soul consists of what Jung called the archetypal intelligence of the Self, together with the power of compassion. The soul is still an individualized entity, but it operates from holocentric, rather than egocentric, principles. The soul slips its higher understandings and sublime feelings through the gaps in the ego, moments in which the censoring agency is off-guard. The soul expresses itself in dreams, in synchronicities, in spontaneous flow states, and in moments of grace that occur when the ego mind is too exhausted to ward off the inundation of blissful love.

But despite such moments, ego-consciousness remains confused and suspicious. How do I know that I am a soul? What does the term even mean? The soul, arriving at the destination of inner silence, recognizes itself as being just as illusory as the ego. The soul is a more subtle illusion, far more profound and serious, but it is finally only the vehicle of an even more vast, inconceivable Presence.

While on the journey toward ultimate Self-realization, the soul functions as a durable power that directs and impels the search toward the Absolute. Soul strengthens the conscious mind, facilitates the exploration of the unknown inner reaches, the space of dreams, of phantasy, of inspiration, of archetypal representations, of all the multiple dissociated realms of consciousness clamoring for recognition. At the moment when the soul has completed its extraordinary journey, it recognizes itself as illusory, a work of the highest art, the creation of a far more sublime Creator. The soul then dissolves into Atman, or Pure Spirit.

Each piece of the psyche claims to be the whole, until it collides with a conflicting piece or encounters a more powerful intelligence, presence, and will to which it must submit. Yet all the pieces together do not make up a whole. The puzzle can never be completed at the level of the ego, or even of soul, simply because they both lack real Essence.

The denial of this fact is the illusory ego's *raison d'etre*. Since it has no true center, but only a swarm of inner usurpers, in the form of superego voices and their programmatic psychic attacks, along with shards of infantile ego images, the ego is in constant chaos, at least at the unconscious levels of the mind—and it can easily break through into a conscious crisis. Each ego and superego fragment retains the holographic property of believing itself to be the 'I'. Brokering their conflicting demands is part of the function of the central censor. But it can only operate according to a rigid program of defending power and prestige, and protecting sources of security and objects of enjoyment. Sometimes, the conscious mind recognizes the illusory nature of its feelings, drives, and attitudes, but still it can rarely over-rule its primitive impulses.

The ego is normally saved from having to realize its weakness and the robotic nature of its pseudo-existence. It escapes self-understanding through willful ignorance and preoccupation with greed, hatred, and the other deadly sins that govern its libidinal economy. Only when all the egoic shards have been silenced is the film of the egoic imaginary finally pierced. Only then, when consciousness recognizes that its egoic identity is no substantial or authentic self, does that empty self-recognition realize the emptiness as the Self.

The ego flees from that recognition, since it feels it as annihilation. Indeed, the Self is void, an absence of objective being, a luminous emptiness that contains all. The Self's emptiness, when understood and accepted, morphs into rapture, an extraordinary kind of love that deserves the adjective 'divine'.

But to the ego, emptiness is the ultimate threat. The ego fears annihilation precisely because it is already non-existent, struggling to mask its pretense of reality from itself and everyone else. So the ego must be continually vigilant, always thinking, always aggressive, always hating, always staying a step ahead of the others. To the ego, this is a cruel and dangerous world in which divine love is an illusion, and because of the ego's emotional fragility, one must reject the other before being rejected.

The ego complex believes it is the entity living your life, until one day its complexities cause it to crash. Its energies will burn out, its passions fade, and its reason for being will collapse in pointlessness and exhaustion. Then, if the ego has the honesty and clarity to surrender to its higher inner power, another more profound center of awareness, the soul, may take over from the censor, and purify the unconscious mind, while filling the conscious mind with what Buddha called *bodhicitta*, compassion and wisdom.

The soul then completes its inner journey to the Source. On reaching the eternal Light, the soul dies into the flame of the immortal Self, known to the ancient yogis as the Atman. The presence of the Atman—the unknown Real Self—emerges gradually within the soul, which intuitively surrenders. The soul makes an offering of all the lower chakras—the power drive, the sexual drive, and finally the security drive—and melts into ecstatic union with the supreme Light of God-consciousness.

There is yet another death still to come, the death of God into the Absolute. This has been called Mahakal, the Death of Death, the final annihilation of all distinction between God, Self, and Universe, and the return to the ultimate Source of Being.

Once the moment of destiny has arrived for the unfoldment of this extraordinary process, the soul—just like the salmon—diverts the ego out of its usual course of existence and incomprehensibly turns toward a strange inner river of Becoming and begins its apparently mad journey into the unknown dimension where completion, death, and fulfillment all wait.

The soul lives in a different dimension than the ego. The ego identifies with the body and thus with the family of the body, with the signature behaviors and personality traits of the biological family, and often with the place in which the body was born. But the soul has a different family, a different life span, and a very different intent. Once the soul is stimulated into activity, it begins to separate from all the known landmarks of the ego, to begin its fateful journey into the inner realms to find its hidden Source—the divine luminous point of pure and timeless awareness that resides as the Heart of all.

Many people have the experience of not being truly seen or understood by their biological family. One day, when the soul awakens, that family begins to appear like an assortment of strangers having no authentic relationship to one's real Being. One begins to separate, at first internally, and then, perhaps, externally as well. The soul comes to connect with its Essence, triggering incredibly heightened aliveness. One opens both heart and mind to one's higher destiny and to the Supreme Love that radiates in its inmost core. This enables it to achieve ultimate fulfillment.

Some souls have to cross the planet on their search; others need only cross the street; while still others can make the inner pilgrimage in the comfort of their own home. This, too, is a matter of destiny. Some people make pilgrimages to Rome or Mecca, others to Jerusalem, Benares, or Lhasa, some to the Congo, Chichen Itza, or Macchu Pichu. Some find in those places what they are looking for, while others have to continue their search. And they may ultimately return to find the treasure was waiting for them all along in their own heart.

What is every soul searching for? The soul is magnetically drawn onward by the unquenchable thirst for its lost Essence—for nothing less than the full realization of God within. At that moment, just as the ego had to die into the soul, now the soul dies into the God-Self, the Atman. And finally, Atman merges into the Absolute. This is known as Jivan Mukti, or liberation-in-life.

The transformation process is no doubt already underway within you. It is useful to those who find themselves in the hands of the living God to understand the nature of the ego, the soul, Atman, and Brahman, the Absolute. Understanding the relationship of all these levels of our Being will facilitate the transition to the deepest level of Presence.

The ego is constructed over a period of years, an ongoing elaborate response to the traumas and demands of infancy and childhood. The soul grows over longer spans of time, often millenia, a durable vehicle that survives the passages between deaths and births, and functions as the psychic creator and container of the ego. The soul is not the Self, and from the perspective of ultimate reality, yes, it is but another illusion. But it is an illusion that we must pass through to gain final liberation.

The soul is constituted by the profound longing for return from the fragility and impermanence of time to the refuge of eternity— yet it keeps moving along the trajectory of linear time, gaining wisdom through the sowing and reaping of karma. Its very identity is woven of the karmic thread that connects all its past and future lives. When that thread comes to an end, when the desires of all those lifetimes of exile in the universe of spacetime, energy, mass, and mind have culminated at last in the exhaustion of its outward-aiming energies, then the soul, like the salmon, seeks its point of origin from which to die back into God in final liberation.

The soul knows when it must begin its journey home. The ego may think the idea is irrational, but it must at some point yield to the higher powers within. You would not be drawn to reading this, if you had not reached the point at which such knowledge/power is unfolding within you. There are probably mixed feelings, of course. But, no doubt, there is a longing for the release of creative energies to fulfill the spirit's ultimate desire. You are on the threshold of that miraculous moment.

Usually there are a number of false starts and dead ends. Until the soul fully separates from the ego, its true desire is always going to be distorted and foiled by the other-directed desires of the ego. The ego has a more limited agenda, a pale imitation of that of the soul. It wants the insignia of power, and more covertly, it seeks to return to the mother's womb and/or receive the father's symbolic phallus. But the ego can never fulfill that phantasy. Sexuality is a mirage. Neither orgasm nor romance can yield the holy grail of wholeness. Climbing the social hierarchy is a fool's game. The ego is doomed to disappointment.

The soul, however, can succeed in its search for a different kind of womb, the cosmic womb, and the phallus of God (in Sanskrit called the *Shiva Lingam*), the penetrating power of the infinite supernal Light. Only in the attainment of the blissful orgasm of ultimate mystical union can the soul at last dissolve. In the moment of its merging with the Light, the soul dies into its own concentrated nucleus of pure Spirit. And then a new kind of life begins.

Just as every salmon finds its own river, and then its own spawning point in that river, every soul must find its own way to salvation. Its moment of awakening and that of its ultimate liberation will be different for each one. For some souls, who were born only a short way up the river of time, the return journey may be easy. But for those who were spawned a long way up the river, the journey home is far more arduous and filled with great obstacles. A few souls were spawned near the very source of the river. They face the greatest difficulties and the greatest rewards.

For those rare souls, the journey will seem endless and will take them through every kind of non-ordinary experience, from the most sublime to the most terrifying, dangerous, and absurd, until the awful moment when the river seems to peter out into a tiny rivulet, and all seems utterly hopeless. At the moment of the deepest darkness of despair, they will at last encounter the spring that is the Source, the luminous loving presence of God. And they will recognize that they have arrived at their journey's end. Now is the season, within the long cycle of planetary time, for the attainment of the supreme goal—for all of us who have been on this long, strange trip.

We are awakening from a trance called history, from being lost in the mists of collective amnesia. For some, these words will provide a shock of recognition. We are returning Home.

PART ONE

Entering the Path

The Transformational Imperative

Like alcoholics at a twelve-step meeting, we must admit the truth: existence has become unmanageable for the human species. At every level, from individual emotional stability to couple and family relationships to global politics, life is in deadlock. There is no solution to our problems—or even the possibility to will a solution—so long as human consciousness remains at its current level of incomplete development. Our conflicted egocentric psychic economy, reflected in our sociopolitical conflicts, must be transcended. Our addiction to the drives and pleasures of the ego—to its nasty attributes like narcissism, greed, hatred, prejudice, aggression, deception, venality, and denial—is destroying our collective existence.

If we are going to survive, we must evolve rapidly to higher levels of consciousness. This has been the deepest yearning of humanity since the dawn of recorded time, the *raison d'etre* of every religion, the message of every great prophet and sage in history. But now our time has run out. We cannot wait for some messiah or avatar or revolutionary movement or benign extraterrestrials or any other form of utopian Other to accomplish the redemption for us. We must do the work of inner transformation ourselves—and do it immediately.

The transformation of consciousness has become THE existential imperative. We either transform now or succumb to extinction. Whether we succeed or fail as an evolutionary experiment will be determined by us, the set of presently existing human beings. And the transformation required can only be achieved one human being at a time. It cannot be mass-produced, although we can accelerate the process by creating a planetary culture that supports this achievement. But someone must go first. We ourselves, each of us who become aware of the imperative, must become role models of the attainment of that supreme ideal.

Each of us must take responsibility for our own inner development—for achieving ego death, followed by sacred rebirth as manifestations of the one Cosmic Self. Out of the illusion that we are many, we must realize we are one—this is the real meaning of the credo on the U.S. dollar bill: *E Pluribus Unum*. What is necessary is not an egoic parody of unity, in the form of submission to empire, or empty new-age nostrums that mask the persistence of infantile ego-systems, but the authentic oneness of the Divine Presence, made possible through rigorous disciplines of self-transformation, meditation, and radical paradigm shift.

It is an ethical imperative that we make the project of self-transformation the top item on our life's agenda. Without the attainment of sacred rebirth into our highest and most genuine potential Selfhood, all else is in vain. We owe such a metamorphosis to our loved ones, to our ancestors and our descendants—but most of all, we owe it to our Self, to the Source of our existence, to the supreme power and intelligence that has created us all.

It is not only a moral but a psychological imperative that we transform now. Unless we do, the dark shadow forces in our psyche will wreak havoc with our emotional stability, if they are not doing so already. As the collective psychic energies on the planet become more chaotic and pathological, the waves of anxiety, paranoia, and despair threaten to overwhelm us. The unshakeable peace and serenity of our inmost Being is our only refuge in such a time. To reach the sheltering energies of the One—our immanent/transcendent God-Self—the ego must first be transfigured, made transparent to the supernal Light that shines from our inner depths.

It can even be said that transformation is a political imperative. Both left and right wing movements have in the past century brought about horrors of mass murder and enslavement. Without a transformation of consciousness, there is no way to overcome systemic corruption, scapegoating, and power-madness. Unfortunately, the left has jumped to the wrong conclusions from Marxist and postmodern insights into the class, gender, race, and other identity conflicts that lie behind the fraying façade of unity characterizing contemporary societies. But political revolution, even were it possible, would not lead to a transformation of consciousness. The same egoic forces win every political battle. The ego itself must be conquered—no other sort of revolution will suffice.

The egoic multitudes that populate today's empires can never attain unity or harmony so long as they remain in the trance of false consciousness. Aggression, deceit, and projection are inherent to the ego. As frustration increases, the paranoid collective ego is prone to psychotic lashing-out as well as suicidal collapse. This is why ever more authoritarian regimes are being imposed, and human rights gradually eliminated. No empire can maintain hegemony for long over the sectarian hordes that are overrunning one failed state after another.

But it should not be overlooked that the ego is inherently schismogenetic. Schisms will eventually break apart every movement, every group, and every governing coalition. Not even spiritual groups are immune to this tendency of egocentric behavior. Only transcendence of the ego can make durable unity possible. There can be no long-term cohesion even within the most rigid sects unless such a revolutionary psycho-spiritual development takes place. Eventually, as Hobbes predicted, egos will be in a state of total war of all against all. Spiritual transformation is imperative because it alone can create a new political event horizon. It alone has the power to potentiate the creative energies that can stimulate a global cultural renaissance.

The current perilous biopolitical situation of human beings is a blessing in disguise. It forces us to do what we would otherwise leave to future generations. But there will be no future human lifetimes on this planet if we do not act now to change the course of our destiny from our present suicidal trajectory toward one that is realigned with the power of love and truth. The current situation also makes clear that real power is not in the hands of the political elites any longer. As the world's political systems devolve, their breakdown is leaving a vacuum. The legitimacy of the old order, the established identificatory alignments, including extended families and religious organizations, is dissolving in dysfunction, in scandal and hypocrisy, in empty ritual and irrelevance.

Many people, unable to contemplate the dizzying possibilities of this period of kaleidoscopic change, remain stunted and stifled in their futile enmeshments with obsolete signifiers of identity and status. The majority has chosen denial as a way of avoiding the anxiety of radical uncertainty. Others have entered a period of spiritual nomadism. They are wandering through a desert of meaningless social activity, or else have embarked upon a determined search for higher understanding, seeking a Star to lead them to a new Bethlehem—some to a manger where they themselves can be reborn as avatars. Some seek new fountains of truth and genuine love. They seek to align themselves with those who display the signs of true worthiness: egoless wisdom, incorruptibility, dispassion, universal love, purity of mind and life, unshakeable inner peace and serenity.

The problem is: life has a long learning curve. Everyone on a spiritual path is growing, aspiring toward the absolute of human perfection, but few have reached it. We stumble on the way, and sometimes we fall. And those we look up to will also fall, from time to time. This recognition of frailty in ourselves and even in our teachers and guides must always keep us humble in our attitude toward others, not judgmental or vengeful, but always forgiving.

Our loyalty to God grows as we learn, and gradually we renounce our temptations as we find the balm of acceptance and healing in God's grace. Because we cannot wait for perfect individuals to appear, we must take the risk to sculpt our own perfection, and to go as far as possible using conscience as our compass, serenity as our barometer, and the wisdom of great sages as our inspiration.

When we meet someone who can take us further on our journey, who can open our eyes to deeper truths and more universal love, we ought not refuse the opportunity to grow. We must gain genuine autonomy, discernment, and inner union with the One Light.

Working through the egoic distortions of our thought processes, fomented by unconscious anxieties, is an extremely difficult undertaking. It is the Great Work, as the alchemists have said, but it must be approached with reverence and trepidation. It is like walking a razor's edge. To have any chance of succeeding, we must learn the art of meekness, yet boldly wield the dagger of Truth.

As Christ has taught us, the meek shall inherit the earth. Communities of those dedicated to the ideal of meekness (a word that derives from Sanskrit via Latin, *mansuetudo*, meaning one whose true Self, *swa*, has conquered his egoic mind, *manas*) are now forming, guided by those with sufficient integrity and equanimity to have transcended at least most of the lower egoic identifications, and who support one another in achieving ever higher development of goodness and spiritual power. They are learning to work together to overcome psychic barriers to developing fearless, truth-seeking, compassionate, holocentric, narcissism-free relationships. Such communities, learning to live in harmony once again with Nature, developing sustainable ecological modes of production and consumption—if they can also maintain ethical and ego-transcendent modes of conscious interbeing—are destined to prosper and provide models for the next age of humanity.

It is imperative that we ourselves become such beings of simplicity and wise living, of pure faith and divine power, not simply worshippers of one or another being who achieved that goal in the past. It is the only way to survive and benefit from this time of troubles, and to be a blessing to others.

We must become Buddhas, not merely Buddhists. We must be avatars of Vishnu and Shiva, not merely Hindus who worship them. We must be Christed, not be content with remaining mere believing Christians. We must become prophets of Allah, not mere proselytizers. We must alchemically transform, not just be scholars of alchemy.

We must metabolize the highest human psycho-spiritual potentials that lie dormant within us, not simply preach or philosophize about that possibility. Our surrender to God must be complete, not mere lip service. Let us use all the tools and insights of every religion, every philosophy, every science, every school of psychoanalysis and therapy to attain this goal. It is necessary to overcome our limited identification with any single religion or ideology and open to receive the wisdom of our entire human heritage of intellectual and spiritual development. We need all the help we can get.

Today, as never before, the physical sciences also converge on the emergent unifying spiritual paradigm to offer support and crucial insights into the processes of transformation and transcendence. Science in past centuries led human consciousness away from the chains of religion. But that was religion that had fallen into degraded and dogmatic misunderstanding of its own mythologically-coded information streams.

Today, every field of science has been revolutionized by the recognition of the necessity to factor in the reality of consciousness. In physics, the most recent mindbending theoretical breakthroughs—mindbending from the Newtonian perspective, but commonplace to realized yogis—in quantum physics and cosmology, yielding such concepts as higher dimensions and parallel universes, relativity, wormholes and time travel, and most importantly, of the fundamental place of consciousness in the constitution of reality—have served to re-legitimize the metaphysics of the Yogis of ancient India.

The same metaphysical insights are at the core of every esoteric tradition, continually reaffirmed by prophets, mystics, and sages of all religions. New understandings in evolutionary biology supporting the concept of intelligent design have even destabilized the neo-darwinian dogma that has limited the scientific imagination to a flattened reductionistic account of reality. The dead-end of materialism is being overcome in minds that had been ideologically hammered into submission for centuries. A renaissance of scientific spirituality is taking place, one that no longer needs to hide in the corners or apologize for its failure to accept the death of God.

Science is re-energizing the spiritual quest. Psychology is helping even more. The overthrow of the old behavioral paradigm that denied the existence or relevance of consciousness has brought the vastness of the unconscious and superconscious realms back into theoretical play in the therapeutic culture wars.

Great efforts are underway to integrate psychoanalysis with the insights of Buddhism and Advaita. Jungian analysis, archetypal and transpersonal psychology movements are all advancing, capturing the hungry imagination of new graduates in the field. Lacanian analysis has triumphed in many of the world's psychoanalytic communities, an approach that unmasks the illusory nature of the ego, and leads to "benign depersonalization," a concept compatible with the nondualist teachings of Eastern spiritual paths. Sullivanian analysis and post-Kohutian approaches are coming to similar understandings.

European poststructural philosophy, extending the work of such thinkers as Husserl, Heidegger, Foucault, Derrida, and Deleuze has also taken a spiritual turn, recharging the field of non-dualist theology. Dazzling thinkers such as Kitaro Nishida, Shinichi Hisamatsu, Keiji Nishitani, and Masao Abe, of the Kyoto School of Zen philosophy, have forged an elegant rapprochement between Buddhism and Western theology and philosophy. God, no longer reduced to an anthropomorphic Other, but now in the formless form of Absolute Nothingness, the unknowable yet immediately present truth of our intelligent self-aware universe, is making a comeback.

We must, of course, ensure that the transformational urge does not become re-appropriated by egoic religion. Sat Yoga is not a religion but a secular set of experimental psycho-spiritual practices. These are protected by ethical parameters that ensure that the results do not become contaminated or misused by the ego. The secular nature of Yoga has led to its adoption as a psycho-technology by all the religions of the East. Meditative practice transcends all possible discursive paradigms. Thus, there are literatures of Shaivite yoga, Vaishnavite yoga, Advaita yoga, Buddhist yoga, and Taoist yoga, to name but a few.

Unfortunately, in the West, the signifier "yoga" has in recent years come popularly to refer to a recent elaboration of one of its preliminary practices, that of *asanas*, the well-known physical stretching and balancing postures, rather than the true aim of yoga, the achievement of *samadhi*—which is the state of pure awareness in which all thought-constructs and other mental noise have been eliminated.

The physical practice of *asanas* played only a small role in the preparatory transformational activities of the original Yogis. Read even a late text like the Yoga Sutras of Patanjali, and you will find little reference to *asanas*. The point of *asana* practice was simply to learn to sit comfortably in order to be able to meditate for long periods without moving. The Yoga Sutras are dedicated to the attainment of *samadhi* and the attendant *siddhis*, the psycho-spiritual powers that come along with advanced mental development.

Today's stunted understanding of Yoga as a form of physical exercise is a symptom of the narcissistic degradation and materialism that have contaminated even the most profound spiritual traditions. The emphasis on physical prowess has led to the unfortunate spectacle of exhibitionistic hatha yogis more proud of their ability to stand on their head than to overturn their ego.

The goal of Sat Yoga is nothing less than the transformation and transcendence of ego-consciousness. Through its practices, we can learn to live in the supramental levels of our Being. Sat Yoga carries forward the work of many modern sages, including Sri Aurobindo, whose integral yoga aims at the downloading of the Supermind into our individual consciousness. The main difference between Sri Aurobindo's effort and our own is that Sat Yoga imports the clinical wisdom gained in the West through a century of psychoanalytic exploration into the praxis of transformation. By applying such skills as symptom and dream analysis in one-to-one atmanology sessions of free associative self-inquiry, while being held in the safety of a positive pranic energy field, yielding the gradual understanding of drives based on subconscious phantasy structures, and promoting a revitalization of cellular energies, the process of transformation is greatly accelerated.

The term *Sat Yoga* means union with our essential noumenal Being. This use of the term Being refers to what is more appropriately called the Ground of Being. It is the fundament of Being that is beyond the dualities of being and non-being, the ultimate Real that no words can adequately explain or describe. Therefore, we sometimes also refer to It as our Supreme Being.

In other words, Sat Yoga is the disciplined practice of living egolessly. Meditation is the core activity of Sat Yoga. Serious practitioners make the time to sit regularly for about an hour at a time twice a day, in addition to occasional retreats in which we sit for eight or ten hours daily, in a state of mental silence, with our whole attention centered on the Self within. Eventually, the tendency to produce egoic thought constructs subsides and the Self

35

emerges in fullness. Our transpersonal identity reveals itself as timeless presence, serenity, love, clarity, wisdom, luminosity, and all-embracing emptiness.

To achieve the ultimate transfiguration, the ego must first be purified. Three overarching vows prove useful: commitment to a simple lifestyle that supports transformation; continual analysis of one's ego dynamics; and daily engagement in benevolent actions that inspire others to bring out the best that is in them. Transubstantiating the ego is the best gift we can offer to humanity.

Human psychological transformation is imperative. Let us quickly do our own inner work and then help as many others as possible. Self-realization is not a luxury for the upper classes. It is the only means of liberation for all beings everywhere. It is also the ultimate adventure. Here is a cause that can be the vehicle of endless creativity, insight, and delight.

To open the heart to the awesome energies of divine love is the sweetest bliss. To live in virtue and nobility of spirit is the most profound satisfaction. To dwell in ceaseless mindful union with the Absolute is an incomparable rapture. Transformation is imperative. It is also our destiny, our timeless *telos* in this cosmic play that is the sport of the Supreme Intelligence. There is a profound urge within us all to realize our oneness with the Creator, the Dreamer of this strange and wondrous dream that is the universe. This urge will manifest spontaneously at some moment. But we can accelerate that occurrence by our efforts to achieve Self-realization. Let us, therefore, enter courageously into the unknown Presence that is the Self, assent to the ascent, the advent of the great adventure: our conscious transformation into the full manifestation of who and what we already are eternally—we have nothing to lose but our suffering.

Overcoming Confusion

One useful way to define the spiritual quest is as a determined effort to emerge from confusion. Many people are utterly perplexed about life, their values and goals, even their identity. As a result, they make bad decisions, fall under negative influences, and suffer from intense anxiety. They usually counter those unpleasant realities by assuming some sort of false mastery or by adopting some superstition or belief system—either a cynical or a religious version—in order to pretend to themselves and to others that they have it together. Unfortunately, the pretense cannot be sustained indefinitely, and the inevitable crash can be devastating.

There is a way out of confusion. It's called self-purification. This is the ancient Yogic advice for the perplexed. It comes down to living in integrity. But it requires attention and discipline. The initial approach is the following: Stop running away from yourself. Simplify your life, spend time meditating in solitude, curb your bad habits, and in general, adopt a more wholesome lifestyle. Do some serious thinking about the meaning of your existence. Start to confront your unconscious behavior patterns. Learn to become a witness to your consciousness.

Once one has gathered the courage to admit one's confusion and get serious about one's life, one still has to overcome a number of false assumptions and voices that will try to engineer a backlash. One of the most common is the belief that, "We are all one, so why shouldn't I participate in the same activities everyone else is doing—the rat race, the parties, the drugs, the alcohol, the impersonal sexual encounters, the mindless sports activity, the aggression, the whole sensual life of the ego—isn't it an egotistic choice to hold myself apart from all that?" This confusion has led to the waste of many lives.

The point is not to "hold oneself apart" from the world, but to recognize that the self one is holding onto is a false construct suffering (for that very reason) from lack and craving. There is a well-known piece of advice that says, don't go shopping for groceries when you're hungry. Your hunger will distort your judgment and you will find later that you have bought a lot of unnecessary and probably unhealthful food. In the same way, it is sound advice not to socialize when your ego is in a state lacking a true center and craving for love, recognition, and grounding. You will end up entangled in a lot of unhealthy relationships.

The fact is that before we can realize our oneness with all that is, we must fully accept our utter aloneness, emptiness, and unfinished individuation. We must complete our process of becoming-different from all others (as well as from our own self-image). We must transform the ego image imposed on us by parents, and overcome the herd mentality and its conventional stupidities, that lock us into an endless struggle for prestige.

One must have the courage to stand alone and speak one's truth. Otherwise, one ends up in egoic enmeshment and self-betrayal, with a broken spirit, rather than a state of integrity. Enmeshment breeds not only confusion, but a sense of unworthiness, insubstantiality, weakness, a desperate need for approval, terror of solitude, and an unbearable lightness of being, to borrow a phrase from the novelist Milan Kundera—in sum, with a need to receive our identity and marching orders from the Other. This always leads to disaster.

Part of the problem is the pace of life today. People keep themselves so busy that there is literally no time left to think, to meditate, to let go and let oneself be. Inner growth requires the ability to wait, to allow the ripening of profound processes and powers that require time and inwardness to germinate within the soul. To wait, like a mother bird sitting upon the eggs in her nest, while inspirations and new clarity incubate within the unconscious, is essential to the fulfillment of our potential.

The philosopher Martin Heidegger, while considering this theme, employed another useful metaphor, that of the woodworker. We need to attune ourselves to our inner processes, the way a skilled woodworker learns to be sensitive to the particularities of each piece of wood. He works it according to the grain, in order to bring out the beauty and strength of the material. We must learn not to live against the grain of our Being. This requires the gradual development of skill and subtlety in the integration of organism, mind, and essence.

One way out of the trap of enmeshment and confusion is to put oneself under spiritual discipline—to dedicate oneself to learning the skills that attune one to Being, to Truth, to compassion, to presence. Such discipline creates integrity. This is optimally achieved with the guidance of a skilled and trusted spiritual teacher. The obstacle is that the ego structure of most people today is extremely fragile and easily hurt by criticism. Therefore, people cannot accept training and shaping and re-forming of their minds and personalities. They find a rigorous critique of the ego's ploys to be unbearable. They do not object to athletic trainers and body shapers, or even cosmetic surgeons, but to undergo soul surgery or re-shaping of the personality is intolerable.

The dominant attitude today of cynical nihilism is another undermining element. You will be warned away from finding help with such words as, "No one has the answers, everyone is lost, don't follow any guru, don't accept any hierarchy, or any value system, you don't need therapy, you can solve your problems yourself, don't show weakness, etc, etc." This attitude cuts off the possibility of receiving help. To overcome this, humility is required.

One must distinguish humility from humiliation, which is always based on toxic shame and a sense of inferiority.

Working with a spiritual teacher who refuses to fall into enmeshment or a master/slave approach to relating can accelerate the attainment of the singularity and universality of one's essence. This is the most direct way to Self-discovery. One can become self-disciplined without the help of a teacher, of course, by keeping such time-tested Yogic vows as non-aggression, non-coveting, truthfulness, cleanliness, and other good habits that promote social peace. One should also practice a daily regimen of meditation. This could be augmented with other uplifting activities (such as playing meditative music, mantra chanting, asanas, pranayamas, chi gung, mindful dancing, etc.). But the ego's skill at self-deception should not be underestimated, and one may find after a long period of such practices that one's egocentricity has not been lessened a bit. What seems like clarity when alone may be revealed as confusion when faced with the coherence of others who are further along on the path. There is no substitute for an intensive process of one-to-one encounters with a trained atmanologist who can pick up projections and pierce through egoic veils until the Self has been realized.

The goal of spiritual discipline is to eliminate confusion, that being the root of our suffering. The only medicine for this dis-ease is transformation of the ego-structure to permit humility and thus recognition of wisdom when it appears in others. Although there is a Zen saying, "when you meet the Buddha on the road, kill him," this must not be taken the wrong way. It is important not to kill those Buddhas prematurely. Learn from them first. Only when everyone on the road, and even the road itself, is recognized as Buddha, and when there is recognition that you also are Buddha, are you ready to act on that saying—by letting others kill you. This requires intense practice of silencing the mind—living in the eternal now, *sans* ego.

One of the most consequential confusions is the confusion of levels. We live in three distinct levels, or registers of consciousness.

We must treat each level in the appropriate manner. There is first the level of *ex*perience—the world of objects and everyday interactions, like that of dealing with bureaucracies, making money, balancing the budget, and buying the groceries. This is also the one level of reality recognized as such by science.

The second level of reality is that of *im*perience—constituted of subjectivity, intuition, spontaneous creativity, aesthetic appreciation, dreams, inspirations, profound and sublime feelings, uncanny energies, joy, wonderment, love, delight—all the aspects of living that make our existence worth the effort. But to many people today, the dimension of imperience has become flattened and inaccessible, as a result of unconscious defense mechanisms intended to ward off anxiety. The price of not feeling anxious is the loss of feeling joyous, loving, and truly, fully, vibrantly alive. Many people go through life wearing a happy-face mask, but behind it they are in despair.

The third level, that of *sum*erience, is this same world of experience and imperience, but seen as it really is, completely freed of the superimposition of thought-forms. Without the knot of the ego holding a false sense of separation between the inner and the outer, the two are realized as one. In that unity, a blissful state of flow ensues, an eternal present. Things happen, chores get done, work is disciplined and accurate, but there is no doer. The dancer has become the dance. It is the serenity of letting all-that-is simply be. In Buddhism, this is referred to as *tathata*, or suchness. This is what Heidegger was pointing toward with his concept of *gelassenheit*, or releasement. It was long known in Taoism as the celebrated *wei-wu-wei*, action that is non-action. This is the key to entering the true Tao that cannot be named or grasped conceptually. In Advaita, this is the essence of karma yoga. All spiritual traditions express similar understandings. There is a universal truth that lies beyond confusion.

To become unconfused, the egoic identity must dissolve, since the ego is confusion itself. To attain trans-egoic awareness, the mind must learn to dwell in silence, or as the Ch'an master Hui Hai put it, to dwell in non-dwelling. When inner silence becomes total, and the grasping, worrying mental operations of the ego have ceased, perception becomes non-dual—the level of sumerience is finally attained.

What is heard, seen, or otherwise sensed is neither external nor internal—it just is. And the endless metamorphosis of what is—the miraculous unfoldment of the Real—is what we are. In the letting go of illusory identification as a separate observer, in fusion with the divine play of the Absolute, in the realization that we have never been anything but the Absolute at play, the emptiness that is form and the form that is emptiness, confusion dissolves in cosmic laughter.

Finding a PURE Path

The ego is a miasma of emotion-tinged thoughts. It is in order to be released from its chaotic swamp of emotional volatility—anxiety, frustration, rage, and depression—that many people begin to seek a spiritual path.

Seekers have traditionally been classified into one of three types. The contemporary Indian sage Sri Ramana Maharshi humorously referred to these classes as gunpowder, dry charcoal, and wet charcoal.

The gunpowder type of seeker is one who, upon hearing spiritual truth or meeting a true teacher, immediately explodes into enlightenment. Such a rare soul is one who has achieved great capacity for discernment between the unreal and the real, is weary of the world and its illusory lures, and is ready to discard the misery of the false egoic identity for the bliss of the true Self.

The second type, the dry charcoal, requires a little more help: some inflammable fire starter, a match, and the company of other hot coals will do the trick. In other words, accurate psycho-spiritual information, a teacher who is on fire with divine love and wisdom, a rigorous practice of meditation, and the support of a healthy spiritual community will make all the difference. In a relatively short time, such a soul will be able to transcend the ego mind and enter into the sacred silence of pure awareness.

The third type, the wet charcoal, needs a far lengthier process of drying out before combustion is possible. Most souls today are of this type, due to a number of factors, ranging from the false assumptions about reality taught in school; the materialist cultural norms; the competitive and pseudo-individualistic egoic milieu; the insecurity and other traumas that are part of most people's upbringing, creating a fear of thinking differently from the herd; and the general fragmentation of the mind that is consequent on an ego-based educational formation.

Many paths will suffice to take one beyond the mire of the false ego identity—particularly for those who are gunpowder or dry charcoal. But for those who are in the wet charcoal condition, a special kind of path is necessary to accelerate the drying-out process. To determine in advance if a particular path can successfully lead such a person to Self-realization, the seeker should make sure that the approach has four characteristics that can be summarized in the acronym PURE.

A PURE path will provide processing, understanding, reunion, and expression.

The initial need is for patient, wise, compassionate *processing* of the unconscious roots of the issues that are causing suffering. There are generally going to be found many layers of unconscious phantasies, assumptions, self-images, superego voices and commands, traumatic energies, hidden censoring agencies and self-attack formations, splitting and projective tendencies, and a host of other defense mechanisms. All of this must be worked through before authentic spiritual insight is possible.

At the same time, a new *understanding* of reality must be cultivated on a conscious level, a map that integrates the repressed unconscious with the transcendent superconscious, the inner with the outer, and the knower with the known. It must be an incisive understanding that will bear scientific scrutiny and is capable of translating every experience into a new key, one that opens the door to the Supreme Reality.

Third, a PURE path is one that will enable authentic and lasting *reunion* with the Absolute, the ultimate attainment of meditation, contemplative prayer, and Self-realization. Reunion with the

Supreme Oneness follows upon the complete emptying out of the ego. Consciousness becomes an utter zero of pure awareness. In this state of simple Presence, the light and love of God emerge as the Ground of Creation.

The final step in a PURE path is creative *expression*, the transformation of the holy eternal moment of supreme union into the Word made flesh. By transmuting the highest truth into form— via poetry, visual art, music, dance, cooking, or other offering of creativity, healing, or charity, the attainment is made palpably real. This has a profound effect on the other coals that are not yet dry or hot, speeding up their process of transfiguration as well. Through the gift of cultural renaissance, the world becomes once more a divine theatre, a place of boundless love and endless celebration, as life was meant to be.

We have all been on an outward path, an impure path, on a long journey away from our origin and transcendent Source. We have trudged through the defiles of time and history, of triumph and defeat, pinned to the wheel of karma in the phenomenal world, until we have reached the endpoint of utter exhaustion. All the hopes and sensual pleasures that this plane of Maya has to offer have been tasted and found lacking. There is no juice in the egoic world any more. It has all become dust in the mouth. There is nothing left for us but to make the journey home. The impure path is done. The PURE path, leading to planetary restoration, must begin. There is little time left to reach the destination.

The purity of the path of Sat Yoga, its practices of meditation and compassionate interaction, of understanding and acceptance, of liberation from egocentric drives, offers a healing vision of realistic hope. And on our return journey to the Self, we bring uncountable riches in the form of raw trauma that will be distilled into the nectar of supreme wisdom earned through hard experience, through falling and rising and falling again, through knowing the dark side and feeling the sting of remorse, through learning the most painful way what is truly important. All the poison we collected will be turned into potent medicine.

In the end, all sense of separation will fall away, leaving only the One Without a Second. We can find that One in a second, when we are ready. And then one becomes a spring of the water of life, a gateway to the Source for all who are thirsty.

This is the way the world ends, not with a whimper, but a double bang: the apocalyptic explosions of the final war that will bring down the titans of Kali Yuga, and the blissful explosion of love and creative power in the hearts of all who realize God.

One final message for those who think they have a right to judge God's methods: Be humble. Surrender. Don't look back. Don't question the unfathomable wisdom of the Creator of the universe. This is how it must be. Out of horror emerges the holy. Empty the mind of every impure thought. Let the Divine Presence fill your consciousness. Trust. The PURE path is a sure path.

The Celestial Revolution

Many people think of themselves as spiritual. But very few seriously consider the possibility of entering into formal advanced spiritual training. In part, this is because there are few serious esoteric spiritual schools in the West. Spirituality has become confused with ordinary exoteric religion, which is centered around ritual, dogma, holy books, guru worship, and either a rigid ascetic lifestyle determined by ecclesiastical authorities, or the opposite, an erotic drugged-out free-for-all without boundaries. It is not strange that people fear being snared by a cult and being manipulated by charlatans. Such nightmare scenarios are the farthest things possible, however, from authentic ethical spiritual training in the Sat Yoga tradition.

Today, there has arisen an unfortunate trend in spiritual education, epitomized by the neo-advaita movement. In such approaches, no formal training is required. One need merely recognize conceptually that the ego is illusory. Their reasoning goes something like this: since the ego is fictional, it does not exist. Therefore, there is no one who requires training. Any effort made in the direction of self-transformation is scorned as supporting the egoic illusion. Gaudapada, Shankara, and Ramana, among the many sages of traditional Advaita, would all have a good laugh at that.

While it is true that dis-identification from egoic identity is the goal, it is not achieved merely through the omnipotent fantasy of wishful thinking. The neo-advaita approach of instant enlightenment through mental edict is part of the problem, not the solution. A mere conceptual recognition of the ego's unreality will be of no avail during moments of severe testing. That is when the neo-advaitin who claims to be realized but has not done the rigorous inner work of purification of the unconscious may be embarrassed by a sudden loss of nerve, a temper tantrum, or a psychosomatic reaction. And without completing such formal training, one will continue to live within the veils of Maya, emitting projections constantly and being affected by, and unconsciously identifying with, the projections of others.

The Advaita tradition historically was linked to the esoteric schools of Yogic training. Once that link was lost, and once yoga itself took a wrong turn into the defiles of the emphasis on physical rather than psycho-spiritual training, the power of Indian spirituality went into decline. Similar deviations have occurred in most other spiritual traditions. That is why it is imperative that spiritual training be revived and restored to its full strength.

The Sat Yoga approach is an effort to do that. This path is multidimensional, consisting of the practice of preliminary methods of relaxation and concentration; meditation; and the attainment of *samadhi*, or egoless presence. In addition, the path explains the value of sustaining the highest ethical parameters for living and for synergizing a transformational community; offers pranic healing as well as nutritional and other health recommendations; provides a foundation for psycho-spiritual understanding (including the ability to analyze one's dreams) in order to work through one's psychic knots, and then to help others with theirs. Sat Yoga also emphasizes the importance of developing aesthetic forms of expression of divine inspiration, filled with the power to transmit the energy of transcendental ecstasies.

Creative spiritual expression—through poetry, dance, music, drama, and other arts—inspires others into the flow of the upper death drive (our inherent urge toward death of the ego and divine rebirth into pure awareness). It can crystallize new forms of becoming for the benefit of all members of the community, thus functioning as a ladder that others can climb to attain Self-realization more easily.

A community that is open to a continual flow of new spiritual forms—new manifestations of the archetype of the One Self—will remain healthy, rather than petrifying. It is when the 'sun door' has been closed, when a society refuses to recognize further prophets, further words (made flesh) from the Logos, when the ideology claims that there was only one son of God or that the last prophet already came and went, that the dogma is set in stone—and then artistic and psychological development goes in another direction, enters the downward flow of the lower death drive (aggressivity and suicidality), and humanity loses its sublime nature and begins to experience its demonic possibilities.

This produces a kali yuga, a time of darkness and degradation, from which we are now emerging (even as our world enters into the deepest depravity, the light of Spirit is dawning anew). The act of separating from the darkness and entering the light is a revolutionary act. Now is the historic moment on this planet for such a Celestial Revolution.

The Sat Yoga approach is designed to support the Celestial Revolution. It involves the following benefits, among others:

- self-discipline;
- skill in maintaining appropriate interpersonal boundaries;
- courage to act gracefully and decisively under pressure;
- balanced judgment;
- diplomacy and non-aggressive assertiveness in the service of the whole;
- augmentation of the capacity for critical thinking;
- integration of open-heartedness and open-mindedness;

- understanding of the congruence of the essence of the world's spiritual traditions;

- knowledge of contemporary scientific thought and its place in a wholistic paradigm of reality;

- purification of the unconscious mind;

- sublimation of base tendencies of egocentricity into divine qualities of compassion, wisdom, spontaneous egoless action, serenity, and patience;

- and other manifestations of spiritual power, including paranormal capacities.

These benefits grow out of the commitment to inner work and Self-knowledge; devoted practice of meditation and contemplative prayer; consistent willingness to challenge oneself to the maximum; and total dedication to serving God in every action.

In any type of human organization, including that of a spiritual school or community, ego conflicts are naturally going to arise among members. The difference between ordinary organizations and a spiritual school is that, in the latter, those conflicts are employed as growth opportunities.

For example, un-transformed egos are inevitably competitive with one another in unhealthy ways. Learning to relate synergistically, free of judgments and one-upmanship, is invaluable to success in life. The underlying obstacle is that everyone wants to be an insider. Egos hate it when they are not 'in the know', when they do not have mastery of the vocabulary, or they are not the favorites of the teacher. This passion for insider status ironically becomes a thick wall that keeps many people from joining discussions in which others are ahead of them in understanding.

Concomitant with the desire for insider status is the terror of coming too much under the influence of a teacher, of losing one's prized sense of autonomy. This is yet another reason one may feign nonchalance about one's spiritual training, and fail to approach it with sufficient seriousness. One may wish to prove one does not really "need" the help of a teacher or spiritual community, that one can "do it alone."

But if one is truthful, the necessity of provisionally suspending one's spurious autonomy in order to evolve into a Self-realized being is clear. In the same way that one must radically suspend one's autonomy during a medical procedure such as surgery, the spiritual surgery of ego-ectomy requires a similar acquiescence to vulnerability. This is the real meaning of discipleship. By being willing to override the impulses of the immature ego in favor of the wise counsel of an adept guide, one can replace omnipotent fantasies with true autonomy.

Many people, even when they have the requisite courage to be physically present in a spiritual training course, nonetheless refuse to speak, even when they have questions, so as to hide their ignorance. This is because they carry toxic shame. Egos hate being judged by others as inferior. So they shield themselves within a shell of shyness. This impedes learning. Unless people are willing to admit their egoic emotions and work through them, they will eventually drop out of this all-important Self-educational process. Without becoming fully conscious of how their egos are sabotaging their own growth, they will leave and join other sorts of groups in which they feel more secure because they can imagine they are on top.

Without humility and the willingness to start at the bottom, however, self-transformation cannot be accomplished. In fact, the working-through of unhealthy competitiveness, inferiority feelings, and shame is the essence of spiritual training. Learning formal knowledge is far less important than facing the internal restrictions upon one's freedom to learn, grow, and interact harmoniously with others. In fact, the transformation of base emotions into pure love and joy, the divine will to create and share, is the most revolutionary act we can perform.

This is why we refer to self-transformation as the Celestial Revolution. It is one of the most delicious of the many fruits of spiritual training. It leads to full 'seven-chakra living'. Life becomes a dance of grace, mutuality, and synergy. This used to be called 'living in seventh heaven'. When lives of beatitude became more rare, that turned into a facetious comment. Now we have become too cynical to even dare imagine the option exists.

But it is a fact that once the egoic issues hidden in the shadows have been flushed out, a delightful *joie de vivre* ensues that remains our constant wavelength of compassionate consciousness. And as one continues on the upward path, the quiet joy becomes ever more intense, until the ego dissolves in rapture. This is what yogis refer to as the Supreme Liberation. It is the final fruit of spiritual training— on the individual level. There are other benefits, of course, ultimately far more important: the effect upon the entire planet of living in the glorious wavelength of divine love. A community of such beings can transform the world.

Without a core group of invincible spiritual warriors—those who have overcome the primitive paranoid impulses of the ego—a healthy spiritual community cannot develop. We have reached a historic moment in which the emergence of synergistic communities of trust is essential to carry humanity forward to the next phase of evolution. The divine energies that the most advanced members of our species are currently downloading need the protection of spiritual communities able to function as 'butterfly farms' for our angelic metamorphosis.

You are invited to join the Celestial Revolution. You too can build your home in the seventh heaven. It is your real estate.

Identity Theft

The problem of identity is an old one in the annals of Western philosophy. Socrates opened the discussion with the hypothetical that, in some variation, still gets thrown at undergraduates. Consider a ship that takes a voyage around the world. At every port, a plank of wood or other element of the ship's structural material is replaced. By the end of the voyage, every bit of the original ship has been replaced—hull, rudder, riggings, anchor, sails, everything. Even the captain and crew have been changed. So the question is, is it the same ship?

If you say no, then you have to deal with the follow-up question of when the ship lost its identity. How much of its material would have to have been changed before you would claim that its original identity had been lost? And then another question would be thrown at you. Would it matter that the ship retains its original name?

If you say it is the same ship, because the new material was put in to restore the original form, and it is the form and name, rather than the matter, that determines identity, then you have to answer new questions: What if the form was modified a little bit? What if a mast was added, or the ship was lengthened a few centimeters? What if the name was changed? Is that decisive?

We could add another wrinkle to the situation: Let's say the ship returns to the same port every evening, after a day-cruise, rather than being on a global voyage. And let us posit that each plank of wood or other part that is removed from the ship is stored in a warehouse, and eventually all the pieces are put back together in the same exact way, so that the ship built in the warehouse and the one on the ocean seem identical. Are they?

Now, of course, we can bring the hypothetical closer to home. Does a girl have the same identity after she has become an adult woman, and all the original matter of her body has been replaced? What if she changes her name? What if she has plastic surgery, a face transplant, fingerprint removal, or even a sex change operation? Will the person have the same identity throughout these alterations? And we can add another question: What if she gets cloned? Does the clone share her identity?

The difference between the identity of a material object and that of a human being is that the human's identity is subjective, not objective. There are many individuals who have conversion experiences and claim that their identity has changed as a result, even without any name or material change having occurred. There are other people who are diagnosed as having multiple personalities, or who are said to be possessed by spirits, or who claim they simply no longer know who they are. There are people who go through the traumatic experience of depersonalization, when consciousness becomes unglued from any sense of being a person at all. And there are the cases of memory loss, ranging from amnesia to Alzheimer's, in which people do not remember their past or sometimes not even the people who are intimately involved in their current lives.

Most people would say memory is the key to identity. They might insist that someone with amnesia or dementia has lost her identity. But possibly that person would say she knows who she is, just not her name, or who others are.

Some link identity to psychological maturity. If an adult suddenly started acting very childishly, clinicians would say he had become 'regressed.' Others might say, 'he's not himself lately.' Has he lost his identity or just certain capacities? Is identity a matter of typical sequences of behavior, or does it have to do with an underlying entity, an essence of some sort—or to use religious language, a soul?

In ancient India, the sages were already debating the issue centuries before Socrates. One question that was common had to do with continuity of identity through reincarnations. If one forgets one's previous life, can we say it was the same soul who transmigrated from one existence to another? And even if one uncovers past life memories, if the traits of body, personality, and even gender, are different from one life to the next, in what sense is one the same being? This question takes on political significance in Tibetan Buddhism. The Dalai Lama claims to be the fourteenth reincarnation of the same entity. But do all Dalai Lamas really share the same identity? What if the next Dalai Lama's identity were to be determined by the Chinese government? Could the matter be proven one way or the other?

The Vedic rishis maintained that the concept of identity itself is a false one. Ultimately, there is only one Self. The whole universe is an expression of the Self. Each apparently separate individual is a fleeting microcosm, an expression or permutation of the One Self. The sages explained how in each lifetime within a cosmic time cycle, some degree of awareness of our ultimate real Identity is lost, and beings in general become more deeply mired in the illusion of false identities that are based on bodily form, rather than the Real of presence. Each soul in the first age of any world cycle lives in a state of universal love and oneness with all that is. But in each subsequent lifetime, some of that original purity is lost, until finally, in their last incarnations, they devolve into narcissistic egos in a permanent identity crisis.

The karmic process, based on the law of entropy, has resulted in identity theft. The original godlike beings that we once were have now become demonic. How could such trashy human specimens even consider the possibility that we were once royal inhabitants in the palaces of the sun king? How to believe that such a solar age even once existed? And even more daunting, how to believe it is possible for humanity to return to that lost state of brilliance, goodness, and infinite love?

The answer may lie in what we can observe in Nature. We could adduce many examples, but the archetypal pattern is that of the butterfly. Does the caterpillar share the same identity as the butterfly? The paradoxical quality of their relationship enchanted the philosophers of ancient Greece, who appropriated the word butterfly, which in Greek is *psyche*, and applied it to the human soul, asserting that we humans have the potential to go through an equivalent metamorphosis.

The difference is that humans were designed with conscious will in place of hard-wired instincts, which give us the ability to halt or deviate from the fulfillment of our evolutionary potential. Once a defensive ego system got installed in our cerebral software, the capacity for spiritual metamorphosis was short-circuited.

Unlike the evolutionary drive of Nature toward ever-greater differentiation, the devolutionary drive of the human ego attempts to maintain homeostasis, ignorance, and self-contraction. In other words, human egos today work at cross-purposes to Nature—in fact, we have become the enemies of Nature. And this has occurred because what we think of today as our identity is actually a case of identity theft.

The Bible clearly states that we are made in the image of God. But the Bible also states that God has no image. In fact, it was a crime in the ancient Israelite religion to make any sort of graven image of God. That is also the case in Islam. The identity of God cannot be defined or objectified or limited in any way. God's identity is not graspable by human reason. But since we are made in the image of the Imageless, the same must be true for our identity.

The Yogis of the East focus upon this imageless and indescribable Real, employing such terms as Brahman (the Absolute), Shunyata (Emptiness), Nirguna (beyond qualities), and Nirvana (beyond vibration). As it is written in the *Tao Te Ching*, the

Tao that can be named is not the true Tao. Even in Hinduism, famous for its multiform iconography, it is clearly stated that the many deities are only metaphors, pointing believers to the One Self that is without form.

Again, let us take Nature as our paradigm. Nature, according to Roman Catholic theology, is both with form (*Natura Naturata*) and without (*Natura Naturans*). The former is Nature in its currently crystallized form. The latter is the intelligence behind Nature's forms. It continuously evolves new forms, but cannot be identified with any of those forms. The wholistic intelligence of *Natura Naturans* originates, sustains, destroys, and transforms life. As a consequence, *Natura Naturata* does not remain crystallized, but evolves. It is an ever-changing flux.

Nature's intelligent Self is perpetually creative, self-transformative, non-egoic, and utterly unlimited and undefinable. Because Nature's wholistic intelligence is incomprehensible from an egoic perspective, such intelligence cannot be proven to exist. The Darwinian idea that human intelligence is a random aberration in a mindless chaos of dumb matter is the very conceit that has driven materialistic humanity toward its own looming extinction. The collective human ego-system has been programmed by the implications of the modern reductionist materialist ideology to collapse into collective psychosis, unable to care about its own species, let alone the welfare of the planet as a whole.

We have paradoxically become the weak link in the chain of Being, the stupid ones who lack consciousness, in a universe that is otherwise conscious. We have become guilty of ecocide, the attempted murder of Nature, through the reckless negligence caused by our colossal narcissism. The vaunted Homo Sapiens has devolved into homos who utterly lack sapience. We have stolen from ourselves our own identity, and now our very existence is being taken from us. The law of karma is fair but stern.

Nonetheless, true identity is that which does not change through time. Identity is our essence, not our form, nor our condition of understanding, nor even our actions. Our essence has to do with our potentiality, and that in turn has to do with our underlying presence—a presence that may be completely unknown to the conscious ego, which flits between future and past, but never finds itself in the present. We attain presence generally only in moments of extreme danger. Sat Yogis are those who have learned, or are in process of learning, to live in the present, at one with our Essence. They are among the few who have chosen egocide over ecocide. The dissolution of egoic consciousness liberates our intelligence from the death that is false self-definition.

Intelligence refuses self-definition, since definition—by definition—is finite, self-limiting, and ultimately non-adaptive. The ego's foolish demand for the hobgoblin of consistency results in an ever-enlarging gap between its mental representations and reality. Its delusion continually deepens, at least until reality forcefully intrudes, ultimately in the form of impending biological failure of the entire species. We have now arrived at that point. Humans are always telling each other we must learn to think outside the box, but why did we create a box in the first place? It is modern human society, rather than Nature, that displays a lack of intelligent design. But what if we were designed precisely this way by the intelligence of Nature to force us to achieve our own higher evolution?

The human ego acts as a limit upon our potential intelligence. The ego is repetitive, since only through repetition can its identity be subjectively maintained. Repetition is antithetical to free will, creativity, and openness to the Real. Therefore, the ego is maladaptive. The human ego is a mental excrescence that serves a function for a limited period of human development, known as childhood, and then should be cast aside, just as the pupa is left behind by the butterfly after it emerges. In a healthy human society, the ego is shed at the appropriate developmental moment, just as a snake sheds its skin.

Rites of passage in traditional societies performed this essential function. But in our demented society, a society that has become lethally petrified, and which is nearing collapse, the ego has become a death mask. It refuses to loosen its grip, strangling the adult's potential for creative living. The ego is meant to be a womb. It has now become the tomb of the human spirit.

Pure, free spirit: that is the closest we can formulate in words our real identity. Once the spirit is free of the encasing of ego, we can soar beyond illusion and suffering, beyond space and time, into the supreme realization of our eternal oneness with the Creator of Nature, the Mother of the Universe: the Absolute.

Fortunately, the intelligence of Nature cannot be defeated by the stupidity of the human ego. She is freeing a sufficient number of her spirit-children from their egoic casings so that once our moribund society of demonic humans has succumbed to the stern law of survival of the fittest, a new community of divinized beings can emerge once more on our planet. Massive geological upheavals will have to occur first, of course, to cleanse the planetary surface. Only a few will survive. Who will make it into the next kingdom of heaven? All religions agree on that: Those with the intelligence and courage to discover their ultimate real Identity. You may be one.

Becoming a Theomorph

Sat Yoga is the science of metabolizing our theomorphic potential. Human beings have the power of re-designing our own psychic structure to exhibit cognitive, ethical, aesthetic, and spiritual perfection. Through the practice of Sat Yoga, we can gain the skills to achieve the full flowering of the Godseed that lies latent within us all.

The inherent powers that become activated in the advanced stages of self-transformation can have tremendous consequences for the phenomenal plane, on the social and political, as well as ecological and geological, levels. This is because gross matter responds to the vibrational transmissions from the subtle energy fields of human presence. This little understood aspect of reality is the key to responding to the challenge of global warming and the other threats we face today. But to bring the power of our vibrational potential into the equation will require full theomorphic transformation.

To be theomorphic implies we have the ability to function as godlike beings. From ancient days, this has been the wager of spiritual science in all its forms—from Hindu, Buddhist, and Taoist Yogas in the East, to Hermetic, alchemical, and kabbalistic esoterism in the West. In the Torah, it is proclaimed as our destiny: "You shall be as gods." Yogis of every stripe have always recognized that the full spectrum of consciousness is available to us. Humans range from the divine to the demonic. But once we drop below a certain point of integrity, we lose the free will to change course. At a given moment, decline becomes fall. Destruction becomes inevitable.

Today, human culture has, as we all know, taken a drastic turn toward the demonic. We have crafted a negative, bloodthirsty, dumbed-down culture that valorizes selfishness, brutality, materialism, ruthlessness, prejudice, narcissism, apathy, unbridled masturbatory sensuality, irresponsibility, ignorance, and paranoia. Unless we transform the culture, humanity is lost.

The demonic qualities that now deform our collective consciousness have led us into a cultural cul-de-sac. Our systems of command and control, out of desperation to maintain power even though they have forfeited their claim to legitimacy, have shifted from primarily ideological and economic methods of seductive recruitment to the overwhelming application of brute force. Ironically, the system can now only maintain itself by destroying itself.

The collective ego system operates beyond the pale of reason. Empires act on the supervening mandate to increase profits, control all valuable resources, collect all possible information, eliminate all perceived enemies, and function in secrecy with no moral limitations upon action. Humans have created monstrous mechanisms of power that, like the fictional Frankenstein, are now bent on destroying their creators. And the need for the system to act in ways that no morally attuned consciousness could permit has led to the elimination of all but the most opportunist and amoral, not to say psychopathic and sociopathic, from most of the centers of power.

We have abused our vaunted intelligence to produce weapons with which we can destroy ourselves utterly and we have put them under the control of those least qualified by wisdom, compassion, and emotional maturity to wield such inconceivably lethal force. Moreover, out of the need to displace the collective anger from being aimed at the system itself, designated enemies are routinely fabricated as objects of hatred, turning civilization into a permanent psychotic war dance.

Our uncaring and insane social policies have led to the karmic blowback of planetary overheating, toxic pollution of the land, water, and the atmosphere, denaturing and contamination of food products, dangerous genetic modification of life forms, and impoverishment of the vast masses of the human population. All these and other foolish policies have put a stranglehold on our capacity to survive. In response to this human stupidity, Gaia, our planet's superhuman intelligence, is bringing about massive geophysical changes to remove what has become a cancer on the biosphere. We are that cancer. We either transform into benign members of the ecosystem or we shall be eliminated.

Here is where our latent theomorphic powers come in. Each of us has the capacity, through commitment to the constant practice of Self-awareness, to overcome the egocentric mentality that has corrupted our character. We can dissolve the identifications and defense mechanisms that veil our essential nature. But we can accomplish this only with discipline and dedication. We must desire wholeheartedly such an extreme makeover, if it is going to occur.

But because our will has become fragmented and dissipated, we need the support of others further along on the theomorphic path. The recipe for success is simple. Work with a spiritual teacher. Participate in a transformational community. Persevere in the reading of inspired texts. Pursue a daily regimen of meditation and dreamwork. Deconstruct resistances. Lead a simple, clean, healthy, ethical lifestyle. Continuously focus on the goal of theomorphic liberation. This commitment in itself requires such humility and seriousness of purpose that few will be attracted to such a path. But there is no other way out of our existential crisis.

Theomorphosis cannot be an ego-driven project. The urge to goodness can only arise from the transcendent Source. Theomorphosis can only succeed if guided by our Buddha-nature (call it Divine Intelligence, the Logos, Shekhinah, the Holy Spirit, or Allah—the name does not matter). In this time of spiritual exhaustion and dire need of redemption, as the tree of life is withering, the power of God has mercifully returned from the long eclipse of history to re-seed the Earth with wisdom and love. With this supreme energy, we have what is necessary to bring about a global renaissance, a new order of the ages.

In this moment, those who seek union with the Ground of Being will become aware of the secret presence of God. The energy is available to overcome the downward pull of the egoic mind, to attain the most precious prize of life: salvation of the soul, the Supreme Liberation, the blissful merging with the transfinite mind of God.

The achievement of theosis will have profound impacts upon everyone in our circles of influence. Once the collective energy field has elevated its vibrational frequency to the critical threshold of global noetic resonance, a massive shift will occur in psycho-ecological interaction, triggering an awesome planetary transformation. Nature will show what She can do.

Planetary conditions are rapidly disintegrating. The crisis will continue to worsen exponentially, until the final tipping point is reached. Then a series of cataclysmic events will bring the current age to a vanishing point. Through extraordinary tectonic processes, our contaminated continents will then sink into the depths and new virgin landmasses will rise from the ocean floor to become accessible for habitation by the few surviving communities. Conditions will gradually become favorable for the inauguration of a new divine culture. This sort of massive planetary transformation has occurred before, and is the subject of the world's oldest myths. Those myths contain more truth than our modern cynical minds ever considered possible.

The present crisis is meant to awaken us from our collective trance. We have forgotten what is real, what is important, what we are, and how we might live in unity. We have lost the path of higher truth and nobility of spirit. The current decomposition of social bonds is making us aware of our mistaken priorities, the lethal nature of our hubris and egocentricity, and the utter contingency and unimportance of our continuing existence, should we choose to remain in our fallen state of arrogance and ignorance.

We have reached the moment of Truth. In the coming collapse of our national and international systems of finance and trade, in the ongoing shattering of our families and social networks, in the rampant paranoia that is ripping apart the matrix of human existence, we have no choice but to realize that we have lost our way. We have lost our Being.

The most important element of the theomorphic project is learning to silence the mind. Only when we have gained sovereignty over our mental agitations can we access and harness the lifegiving energies of Presence.

To achieve this goal, we must renounce distractions. We must give up judgments and opinions, limited loyalties, attachments, and projections. We must interiorize our awareness, renounce self-images and concepts, and retreat into our inmost Essence. In the attainment of emptiness, we come upon the astonishing realization that what we had considered the external world is nothing but the manifestation of the Absolute. The dynamic impermanence of the world process is the eternal play of divine energies in the creative expression of infinite wisdom. Human history is but a cosmic cautionary tale of what happens when we forget who we are. Once we learn again to speak the language of God, life will transcend the apparent barrier of death and become an endless delight.

One life ends, another begins. One age dies, another is born. The environmental crisis is not an inconvenient truth, after all, but rather, the harbinger of the most wonderful Advent possible. The cyclic nature of temporal reality was common currency in the ancient world. It became part of the patrimony of our cultural intelligence that we for centuries took for granted. It is as much a part of Greek and Roman understanding as of the East. Knowledge of the eternal return is part of the perennial philosophy, embedded in the esoteric dimension of every world religion.

What all the great religions prophesy—apocalypse, redemption, the return of the gods, the coming of a new kingdom of heaven on Earth—is now about to come to pass in the most unexpected way—a way that will befuddle most believers of those religions even as the prophecies are being fulfilled. This is because modern religious leaders have misunderstood their own symbols, have taken their metaphors too concretely, and have misinterpreted their founders' teachings according to egoic wishes rather than transcendent wisdom.

Yet the great sayings are true. The savior will come as a thief in the night. We need to prepare ourselves for the descent of grace and liberation. God became man that men may become gods. The true Passover is yet to be observed. Build thee an ark, a *merkabah*, a lotus life, to float above the Flood. Cleave to Allah. The hour of judgment is nigh. As Buddha says, work out your salvation with diligence. Become a Theomorph.

The Basic Practice

The basic practice of Sat Yoga is very simple: Just Be. What could be easier? There is literally nothing to do. Meditation is a state of utter repose. Why do so many people find this difficult? If we understand the answer to that, then we are halfway to Liberation. So let us analyze the nature of the obstacles we must surmount.

The reason that simple advice like "just Be" is not sufficient to enable most people to gain spiritual Liberation is that 'normal' ego-consciousness is completely out of touch with our Being. (We are sometimes writing Being and Be with a capital letter to indicate that we are not referring to our egoic sense of being, but to the Ground of that being, the primal awareness that encompasses our mental consciousness.)

We cannot even properly understand the word 'Being' since the egoic mind has never experienced it. The mind tends to distort the concept of Being to signify regression to primitive ego states, rather than transcendence of the ego and its illusory charade of being. This egoic self-deception explains why the traditional approaches to Self-realization, based on such simple formulae as 'Be here now' or the classic mantras like 'thou art That' or 'I am Brahman' are difficult to comprehend. Our minds have become too externalized, body-identified, and word-addicted to apperceive the true nature of what is being signified.

Our existence has become identified as a body that thinks. The famous formula of Descartes, "I think, therefore I am," is symptomatic of the problem. In fact, now the situation is even worse, for we have become more image-identified than symbol-identified. Today, a philosopher might assert, "I see myself in the mirror, therefore I am." We have so lost touch with our Being that we can only demonstrate to ourselves that *we are* by seeing ourselves being seen in the gaze of another. In fact, some of us are so insecure that we must assure ourselves of being by dominating another being, if not as many other beings as possible.

At a second level, we assure ourselves of existing by representing our being in language. We must emit thoughts constantly. These must be thoughts of self-justification, if not self-aggrandizement. But thinking fails to ensure being. In fact, mental agitation only obscures our Being. Descartes would have come closer to the truth if he had argued, "Because I think compulsively, and my mind is constantly full of chatter, I have become unaware of my underlying Being."

So the phrase 'just Be' means: stop thinking. Only when we halt the production of mental constructs can we recover the awareness of Being. This is easier said than done, of course. We are thought-addicts. No matter how banal and irrelevant the thought, most of us prefer a mind filled with words and images than a mind that is empty and fully present. This is a strange phenomenon. We cannot seem to rest in a state of inner silence and serenity, unless we first exhaust ourselves physically or trick ourselves with absorption in some external activity. Another method is to adopt an auxiliary ego to do the thinking for us, as happens when we fall into a hypnotic trance or follow a guided meditation. This yields temporary results, but at the cost of long-term dependency. Liberation requires self-induced mental repose.

The power to control the mind, to bring the mind to inner silence on command, is the key to success even in mundane fields. Without that power, we are crippled. If we cannot concentrate, we cannot learn. Our creativity, our perseverance, our ability to listen to others, will all suffer. Our lives will remain trapped in a very small, narcissistic box. So, why is the ego so averse to gaining peace of mind?

The ego is in an underlying condition of desperation, like a dog chasing its own tail. It is trying to catch itself, to grasp who and what it is. Therefore, most egos feel a powerful urge to stare into mirrors. And many relationships are formed in order to control the other's image of us through a variety of psychological maneuvers.

Of course, all those efforts of control are futile, since the ego knows in its heart that the self-image is false. And thus behind its brave front, the ego dwells in a permanent state of anxiety. When one enters the spiritual path, one deliberately intends to give up of the egoic front as well as the futile chase to attain union with the self-image. Liberation begins with realizing the unattainability of the Self. You cannot catch your tail. But your tail is part of you. You don't need to catch it. You *are* it. You *are* the Self. Therefore: 'Just Be.'

Of course, those words can only be heard correctly by those with ears to hear—those who have overcome the tendency to allow themselves to be seduced by the passions of the lower chakras. 'Just Be' does not mean to give oneself over to the unholy desires of the ego. The lower-chakra drive energies must be re-channelled, converted into wisdom, love, and higher will, into the power to digest the shadow, to transform the psychic structure, the hatred and the dread that lie at the core of our unconscious, and to accept the truth of our radical aloneness.

Since our Being is absent as an object in egoic consciousness, every attempt to reify it conceptually or imagistically must fail. Whatever we think we are cannot capture the essence that is aware of the thinking of that thought. Awareness escapes all nets that our minds fashion in which to capture it. Our essence of presence is pure freedom. This freedom is so radical that we ourselves cannot possess it.

In other words, we cannot know, either with the senses or with thoughts, who or what we are. The Self is unattainable as an object of knowledge. We cannot know the Self in someone else, either. This is why egoic relationship is impossible. It is based on flawed assumptions and projections. Therefore, relationships generally end in frustration and impasse. Friendships often petrify into ritualized transactions lacking depth. Marriages tend to become either endless, angry tirades or cold, inert nights of the living dead. Authentic, loving relationships can only happen in the realization of our interBeing.

These dead-end egoic dynamics occur not only at the individual and family levels, but at every level of existence, including that of national and international (non-)relations. This is the core problem that is paralyzing the human race. Either we find a way to surmount the loveless power-hunger of the ego or we will be destroyed by its collective death drive.

The practice of Sat Yoga is a way to escape this trap. It begins with the realization that few of us know our essential nature. We are in exile from our real Being. To understand that Self-ignorance is inherent to 'normal' ego-consciousness is already to advance.

To grasp fully the significance of the statement "I cannot know who I am," is to confront the illusions of narcissism. We must come to recognize that all self-images and concepts are false. The Real Self is formless presence. To realize that Emptiness, which is another term for the repose in which self-unknowability turns into presence, is our true nature, frees us from having to put up a false front. It eliminates anxiety. Then we can take the next step: to realize the emptiness of Emptiness. In other words, there is no ego there to experience its Emptiness. Even the 'I' that comments on this is illusory. Thus, there is no infinite regress of 'I' after 'I' after 'I', each one reflecting on the emptiness of the previous one. There is no objective 'I' and never has been. The 'I' is only a trick of language. Yet, once the search for an objective 'I' is given up, once and for all time, the Self is realized as eternally present. The Self IS, beyond the plane of representation.

The illusion of an objective 'I' is a necessary part of socialization. It is a convenient fiction that enables the installation of psychic structuring—behavioral norms, values, ideals, and the like—in our children, to inculcate in them positive ambitions that further their education and adaptation to social rules and enhance their ability to differentiate themselves from the herd. But once a person can stand alone and think independently, the illusion of the ego-self must be transcended. In traditional societies, there were spiritual teachers, gurus, shamans, rites of passage, and mystery events to help people attain ego transcendence and Self-realization. Today, our religions and therapies are failing to help cut the egoic umbilical cord, the psychic operation that alone can turn those who are physically adults but psychologically still children into true adults. Sat Yoga performs that essential function.

Once the mind gains the capacity to stop producing I-laced thoughts, there is an awakening from the egoic trance. At that point, both sides of the subject/object duality fall away. Not only does the objectification of subjectivity come to an end. Simultaneously, what had been perceived as the world of objects is recognized as the astonishing expression of the One Self. Of course, the psychological tendencies of the ego may not vanish automatically or immediately, but they can now be worked through without internal resistance.

In Mahayana Buddhist terms, there is the double realization that "nirvana is samsara," and "samsara is nirvana." Or: emptiness is form, and form is emptiness. In Kashmir Shaivism, the teachings offer the double realization that 'I am Shiva, the Supreme Self', and 'I, Shiva, have become the universe'. In Advaita, it is taught that, 'I am Brahman', the Absolute. The world is mis-perceived as a separate material reality. This is Maya, illusion. But once liberated from Maya, the Atman (the individualized microcosm of the Absolute) recognizes both itself and its world as nothing other than

Brahman. All the different schools of Eastern wisdom come finally to the same understanding of the indescribable Ultimate Real, though approaching our Supreme Being from different angles, ranging from the ontological to the epistemological to the phenomenological. The same is true of our Western monotheistic religions, at least in their esoteric levels.

But when we consider such a statement as "I am Shiva" or "I am Brahman" or "I am That," we must keep clearly in mind the non-dual significance of such an equation. It is not the case that there is a personal 'I' identified with a body and a name and a history that has the property of being infinite light and love. Rather, what must be realized is that there is only infinite luminous, loveful awareness, and that this rapturous awareness, rather than a human person, is the reality behind the misunderstood word 'I'.

Thus, Sat Yoga offers nothing new or different from the understanding that has always been taught, in every culture, by those who have realized the Absolute Self. The only word of caution is to beware of confusing levels. Do not identify the Supreme Being with a person who claims to have realized the Supreme Being. The 'I' of the statement is never the Real I.

The only way to escape the egoic illusion is deep understanding and discernment, gained through constant practice, constant return to the Emptiness that is the Self, and continuous recognition of the Presence of the Absolute, encompassing and illumining the personal identity.

In the famous sculpture of Nataraja, the Lord of the Dance, the Absolute, in the form of Shiva, is shown in an eternal dance on the head of a dreaming dwarf that represents the human ego. Awakening is the simple realization that the dwarf is the egoic thinking process, and Shiva the beautiful egoless reality of non-thinking Presence. This is a powerful visual equivalent of the ancient formula, 'I am *That*'.

In other words: Just *Be*.

Seven Commitments of a Sat Yogi

People tend to feel a lot of attachment to their clothing. But when even your favorite outfit no longer fits, and you realize that you will probably never be able to wear it again, then most likely you'll be willing to give it away, if only to make space in your closet for new clothes.

The same thing can happen with your ego. One day it will become too small for you. The problem is, you may not know how to get it off. Besides, you are probably afraid of appearing in public naked. That is the time you can use the help of a good spiritual guide to tailor for you a new approach to being.

When one outgrows the ego, one enters a strange new dimension. The greater your enthusiasm for transcendence, the more drastic will be the response of the egoic powers within and without. To realize the Self is to lay down the gauntlet to Maya, the agency of cosmic illusion, and to the egoic censoring agency within the unconscious. The censor will send its strong-arm agent, the superego, to threaten and abuse you. They will throw all they have at you in order to scare you back into 'normal' ego consciousness. This is the point at which one must take up the sword of the spiritual warrior. Great seriousness of purpose is called for. Use the sword of truth to cut through the spider web of attacking thoughts. If you do not accept the ego clothing voluntarily, it will try to force itself on you like a straitjacket. But if you recognize its illusory nature, and refuse to be intimidated, you will discover that it has no power over you.

Most people give in to the intimidation of the superego. They hedge their bets. They sabotage their spiritual unfoldment to satisfy the superego's demands. But then they try to perform religious rituals or pray, or meditate, to undo the damage. This approach does not usually work. You cannot keep one foot in each of two boats that are slowly moving apart on the ocean. You must at some point make a choice. That is the point of no return.

It may mean giving up cherished illusions about any of the following: finding the perfect mate (or at least sleeping with the most attractive lover); winning the maximum profit in business, or seducing Lady Luck at the casino; or making things perfect in one's family (the famous rescue fantasy) by sacrificing one's own happiness. It means making the difficult choice to truly grow up (on the inside) and fly on one's own. It means separating emotionally from enmeshment with others. It means accepting fully the reality of inner solitude. It means living without the illusion of a safety net.

In the beginning stages of one's new life, there will naturally be moments of doubt and occasional falls. But one must get up, dust oneself off, and continue onward toward freedom. Without vowing wholeheartedly again and again to remain fully committed to life lived in truth, as pure awareness liberated from illusions, one's powers of discernment will not function effectively. To whatever extent one backtracks from the desire for Self-realization, one will encounter the whiplash of instant karma. The universe will no longer allow halfway measures.

In order to protect yourself against lapses that can result in nasty falls into the anguish of egoic delusion, and the inevitable hangovers that follow, you would do well to establish a regimen that keeps your existence operating within optimal parameters.

For this purpose, seven commitments are suggested:

- a commitment to daily sitting meditation—at least 40 minutes in the early morning and another session in the evening;
- a commitment to daily reading of uplifting and insightful psychological, philosophical, and spiritual texts—to keep

one's mind on a high wavelength, focused on the sublime goal of Self-realization;

- a commitment to a healthy lifestyle, to moderate consumption of sattvic food, daily exercise, and avoidance of abuse of alcohol, drugs, television, internet, social or sexual encounters that dissipate one's energies and betray one's highest purposes or integrity of Being;

- a commitment to radical truthfulness;

- a commitment to continuous deepening of one's understanding and capacity for love—through frequent meetings and heartfelt conversations with one's spiritual guide, the supportive company of others on the spiritual path, volunteering to serve one's spiritual community altruistically, and taking meditative retreats whenever possible;

- a commitment to processing and working through all symptoms, all forms of acting-out and acting-in, as well as one's dreams and other manifestations of the unconscious;

- a commitment to achieving complete inner silence, serenity, and blissful union with the Supreme Self.

These commitments will produce extraordinary effects in your life. Any interest in mundane things will fall away naturally. Equanimity, psychological maturity, wholeness, egoless and joyful creativity will soon become your ongoing state. You will cope effortlessly with all the changes that the world is undergoing, recognizing them as the birth contractions of the coming age of higher consciousness.

Your every thought will be a blessing, every word a benediction, and every act an outpouring of grace. And your light-filled life will be its own beatific reward. God is eternally present as your Self.

Remember: Every commitment you make to God is fully reciprocated.

The Agony and the Ecstasy

Entering a spiritual process is equivalent to agreeing to undergo an ordeal. Carrot juice is delicious, but if you are the carrot, you may not be so eager for it. To drink what the Taoist alchemists call the elixir of immortality, all that is mortal and false within your consciousness must first be juiced like a carrot. The processing of the ego leads to the ecstasy of liberation, but there is no avoiding the agony that must precede it.

In Sat Yoga, we speak of the Triple Agony. There is the agony of the practices, the agony of the insights, and the agony of the impossible object.

Everyone is cognizant of the agony of the practices. The core practice is meditation, and for many it is in the beginning sheer agony to sit 'doing nothing' but attempting to silence the chaotic mind. Much of the agony comes at first from the sense of failure, of realizing time and again that the mind cannot be held still, but wanders off with you wherever it chooses—or worse, it puts you to sleep.

But persistent efforts lead to a deeper realization—that unthought agonies have been hiding in the unconscious layers of the mind—and that the chattering and sleeping were only defense mechanisms against uncovering those veiled psychic traumas. Because of their unbearable nature, the assistance of an adept spiritual guide is useful to ensure the success of the karmic purification process. But the need to admit needing help can be another agony.

The path of Sat Yoga involves making some threshold life changes that can also seem like agony. These changes are often formulated as vows of living according to the mandate of strict ethical practices and self-restraints. They are traditionally called *yamas* and *niyamas*. The *yamas* include vowing never to act out, never to speak cruelly or aggressively to another, or to be violent, or to cut off relationships without an attempt at understanding and compassionate reconciliation. And of course that includes vowing to eliminate unconscious aggression, otherwise known as passive aggression, which includes such maladaptive behavior as not keeping commitments, coming late to appointments, distorting perceptions, mis-remembering events, or other forms of subtle sabotage and irresponsibility.

The *yamas* also include a vow not to use sexuality inappropriately. One ought not use sex as an outlet for aggression, or to turn another being into an object of conquest, possession, or cheap thrills. Another vow is not to escape from clear awareness through the drinking of alcohol or taking drugs or through spacing out in front of a TV or computer screen. Another *yama* is to be truthful. Yet another is not to steal or even to covet the possessions or status of anyone. All these vows can be agony at times, and their value may only be recognized after a long period of struggle. But they will keep your life on track until the higher intelligence obstructed by the ego emerges into full consciousness.

Likewise, the *niyamas* can be an agony. They are principles of positive behavior, rather than constraints. They include: maintaining internal and external purity (physical hygiene as well as the refusal to be stained by ugly feelings and thoughts); contentment (the reduction of desires and the cultivation of serenity); austerity (simplicity and self-discipline, endurance of adversity without complaint); and daily study of the wise words of illumined sages. These practices can all be inconvenient at times, but the habits of thought and behavior they bring about are worth their weight in gold. All human civilization and culture worth defending are based on such principles and practices. They constitute the essence of religion.

The agonies that surface as a product of dedication to the practices have to do with the torsion they work upon our ordinary search for meaning in life. The ego seeks meaning in its tasks, its talents, its worldly accomplishments, and its family ties. But all of those, as the prophet saith, are vanity and a striving to catch the wind. Meaning can only arise as a product of character, and meaning itself is only a bridge to transindividual, transfinite Being. The ego has no Being. That is its ultimate agony—not the trauma of feeling unloveable but of lacking any reality at all—and only the character strength to admit that lack of substance, our utter groundlessness, will keep one on the path through the dark nights of the soul that must be encountered on the night sea journey into nothingness that all of us must sooner or later undertake.

Ironically, it turns out that all the egoic desires we must curb with such difficulty in the beginning of our transformational efforts turn out not to be our true desires after all. Everything the ego thinks it wants was installed as programming by parents, teachers, peer pressure, the media, and the various ideological codes of society—or else is the residue of repressed infantile wishes that no longer serve us as mature beings. Once that psychic detritus has been removed, we realize that our original nature is our true nature, and the desire with which we were born remains the only one that moves us: to live in free, spontaneous, joyous oneness with the universe.

On the way toward this ecstatic realization, the agony of the practices is accompanied by the agony of the insights. The final vow of the first agony leads into the second agony: the study of the words of illumined sages will lead to insights that at first can be extremely difficult to hold onto. The words of true wisdom are not retained by the egoic intellect. They seem at one moment lucid and obvious, but a moment later, one realizes how slippery, elusive, and out of reach they are.

Just as dreams tend to slip away only moments after waking up from sleep, ideas that come from the higher planes cannot be easily fixed in the mind. This is why we must study these ideas every day. The reason they are so elusive is that they do not fit into the dualistic logic of the egoic mind; they cannot be categorized or dropped neatly into our usual boxes and filed away. If the egoic intellect were to really internalize the core ideas that constitute the greatest wisdom, those realizations would act as an acid that would eat away the egoic mind in no time. So instead, the ideas are dropped like a hot potato. Wisdom is agony.

The final agony on the spiritual path is the agony of the impossible object. The impossible object refers to that which is represented by the alchemist, the magus, the guide or guru on this inner journey who will sometimes seem to the aspirant (who labors under the spell of projections and the false pride of the egoic narrative) to be the obstacle or even the enemy.

The relationship between spiritual teacher and student is unique and impossibly mind-boggling. The student's ego will try to fit the relationship into one of the usual boxes, and to turn the teacher into some sort of known quantity that can be mastered and eventually belittled and cast aside as useless. The teacher may be fantasied as a sex object, a friend, a devil or a god—but so long as the ego's veils remain in place, never truly seen or understood. But in the process of confronting the frustrating life koans produced by this surreal relationship, we come to know ourselves ever more deeply. Our old egoic self-representations cannot survive this encounter. Ultimately, all representations prove inadequate. At some point, the agony of the ego narrative gives up the ghost, and a magical moment of satori supervenes. Words are replaced thereafter by the delightful sound of cosmic laughter.

Spiritual guides have the unenviable task of preventing their students from becoming mere followers (which is what the egos of the students would love to remain, in order later to morph into rebels). Since the goal of all true inner work requires first the attainment of mature egoic individuation—which includes the capacity to think for oneself, to act from an internal locus of empowerment, and to be free from emotional dependency or enmeshment with an Other—the true teacher must remain a paradoxical figure, one who is impossible to possess, coerce, manipulate, or imitate. The student is to be led to independence, not submission. But it would be an error to settle for rebellion rather than becoming a true revolutionary.

What is required for navigating through the ordeal of an uncanny and impossible Other is the creation of a radically new kind of relationship—a transformational relationship—which is not an ego-to-ego relation, but a nondual relation, a relation of love that does not become perverted into desire or deceitful soothing; a sacred relation, a commitment to the search for truth, no matter how much it hurts; a commitment to the continuing analysis of why it hurts, when it does, and to continuing dialogue and self-enquiry until the root of all trauma has been uncovered and healed through understanding, empathy, and energetic transmission.

The successful student must have the integrity and character to maintain the sacredness of the relationship with the teacher, not trashing it by complaining about it to others (who cannot understand) or allowing others to influence one's attitudes or weaken one's resolve. The transformational relationship must be kept a hermetically sealed vessel, if the ultimate metamorphosis of consciousness into divine crystallization is to be achieved. The agony of the relationship to the impossible object must be protected at all costs, because it is the essential agony that will transmute all agonies into ecstasy. And throughout the relationship with the external guide, it is essential to remember that the outer guru is but a representation of the inner guru, who is the true impossible object, because it is the Self.

The paradoxical and perplexing nature of the work of the spiritual teacher was clearly portrayed long ago by Lao Tzu in the *Tao Te Ching*:

The Master leads
by emptying people's minds
and filling their cores,
by weakening their ambition
and toughening their resolve.
He helps people lose everything
they know, everything they desire,
and creates confusion
in those who think that they know.

In more modern psychoanalytic terms, the teacher must permit the projections of the bad object to emerge (by avoiding egoic collusion) and allow the student to feel the power of the affects that accompany their projections. The student must witness how quickly love turns to hate, how easily the guide can shift from seeming to be a god to a devil and back to godhood, and in general how thoroughly the mind is under the power of black-and-white affects and projections.

The student must consciously work with the repressed terror of abandonment and the hatred of the other who refuses the demand for fusion. The student must face the fear of aloneness and solitude. The student must also work through the opposite fear of losing autonomy, of becoming a mere extension of the other, of being a fool for having trusted another, for taking the risk of becoming vulnerable. And the student must be willing to stick through those awful moments until the realization breaks through that the teacher is neither god nor devil, and that what had been taken as mortal torments to the ego were profound teachings, the necessary trials that mature into true transfigurations.

Is the process worth all this agony? We must each answer that for ourselves. But what is clear is that once the process has reached its culmination, once all projections have been dissolved, once a stainless character of nobility has been built, once the mind has been self-mastered, once the energies of affect have been contained and transmuted into their purest form, the agonies do turn into ecstasies.

The triple ecstasy consists of deliverance of the true essence of our Being; the attainment of unshakeable serenity, pure awareness, and intelligence free of illusion; freedom from fear or craving; and the ultimate delight of union with the Supreme Self, the source and energy that manifests all that is.

It is up to each of us to determine the value of such ecstasies. As awful as are the agonies of the spiritual path, the agony of life lived behind the blinders of the ego are of another register altogether. And those agonies are not followed by ecstasy, but offer only momentary discharges of tension, minor thrills and orgasms, followed by ever deeper disappointment and despair. One must weigh the options carefully, since not only life, but eternity, lies in the balance.

Once the choice has been made with mature realism and full commitment, one's perspective on all events instantly shifts. And suddenly, what had been a triple agony only a moment before becomes an ecstasy forever.

PART TWO
Awakening

Enlightenment or Crack-Up: Choose

Each of us, until the inner purification process has been completed, is filled with tensions and conflicts. When those are resolved, anxiety will be converted to serenity. Until then, peace and integrity remain out of reach. But doing the difficult work of inner exploration and transformation requires a level of maturity, perseverance, and passion for truth that are generally not possible except to those who have already resolved their inner conflicts. This is the Catch-22 upon which most efforts of self-transformation founder.

The result is that most people cope with their conflicts through employing a pastiche of less-than-optimal defense mechanisms. These range from the ingestion of mood-altering substances (including anti-depression and anti-anxiety medications) to the more primitive methods of projection, denial, hyperactivity, schizoid withdrawal, obsessions and compulsions, hysteria, delusions, and the rest of the well-known panoply of egoic maneuvers.

If those tactics worked, it would be useless to raise objections. Only a few finicky philosophers would contend that truth is preferable to illusion, since truth is so much harder to bear. But the problem for those who choose illusion is that the benefits do not last. In the long run, difficulties multiply when one chooses pathology over truth. It is still the case that only the truth can set us free.

The question remains how we gain the discernment and the strength necessary to process our psychic pain and finally attain serenity. If the ends are to be healthy, then the means must also be healthy. This is why we do not recommend blind submission to an external authority (the usual method to achieve a *faux* equanimity, which keeps the social hierarchies in business). Real serenity requires something more substantial: enlightenment.

Of course, many will laugh at the idea that enlightenment is something substantial. But the term means returning to our innermost substance, the essence and ground of our Being. Nothing less than return to the source of our Being will overcome the pathologies of the false self. Of course, we must understand the term substance not as an objective entity, which it has come to mean in Western philosophic discourse, but rather as the ultimate sub-stance, that indescribable non-objective absolute which stands beneath all that we think is real, beneath all our edifices of thought, all our paradigms of reality. Substance is therefore no-substance, being different from whatever appears in the world and whatever we can conceive about the world or the self. This is the significance of the Advaita concept of Brahman and the Buddhist concept of Emptiness, or *Shunyata*. This is the realization that constitutes enlightenment.

The approach to enlightenment that is most highly recommended involves developing our capacity to reason, so that we attain clarity regarding the impotence of reason to grasp the Real—and recognize the need to transcend the dimension of thought. We need to think clearly for lesser reasons as well: to attain psychological maturity and intra-subjective discernment, to be able to translate our feelings and intuitions into symbolic thought, to apperceive when we are not being true to ourselves, or to others.

It also helps to understand the dynamics of the unconscious. If this is accompanied by refined meta-communication skills to maintain integrity and balance in relationships with others, then most of our suffering, caused by the phantasies and manipulations of the ego, will be resolved, and the way is clear for the realization of the Self. Transcending ego-identification becomes easier when the mind functions at a high level of self-understanding. Clear thinking that includes what is now referred to as high emotional intelligence eliminates the need for the more primitive defense mechanisms.

Today, the world is going in the opposite direction. Rather than moving toward enlightenment, society is falling into utter darkness and brutality. People are losing the capacity for both love and critical thinking. There is an epidemic of attention disorders, learning disabilities, depression, and other pathologies of mind, as well as psychopathic heartlessness, that are making inaccessible the highest potentials of human intelligence and character.

Ironically, today more than ever before, we are dependent on a work force with a high level of emotional maturity and stability to keep society functioning. Air traffic controllers, pilots, nuclear plant technicians, surgeons, nurses, electrical engineers, bus drivers, and so many other professionals need inner peace, concentration skills, and emotional stability in order not to make mistakes that could be catastrophic. In every field, the thinking function, equanimity, and the capacity to cooperate are essential. For one to work successfully, one must be able to accept rational, constructive criticism. But business owners are discovering ever more often that employees will no longer stand for criticism. Some quit, others react with passive-aggression or outright insubordination.

The ego structure of most human beings at present simply cannot tolerate correction. Therefore, people are losing their capacity to learn. At the moment when they are needed more than ever, our human resources are short-circuiting. Moreover, societies are making the problem worse by imprisoning young people (often for victimless crimes) in unbelievably high numbers. Wars are also depleting social capital. When a nation sends its young people off to war, a high percentage of the survivors return home with grave psychological disorders. Prisons and armies are psychosis factories. They create disturbances that gravely erode the cohesion of society. At the upper levels of society, there is even greater disturbance in the form of corruption and unfair social policies. The fundamental social contract is effectively being nullified.

The problem of incorrigibility is more acute than ever among children who are growing up today. Parents are finding that schools simply can no longer educate children. They cannot discipline them. The children refuse to accept authority figures. They are responding to the vibrations of the collective unconscious, and they have already rejected higher social values before they can tie their shoes. The problem is exacerbated by the fact that most private schools are more concerned with their financial bottom line than with the successful molding of children's character. And the resources of most public schools are woefully inadequate.

In general, the human ego structure is becoming more fragile, narcissistic, and antisocial at an alarming and accelerating rate. This is abetted by the fact that nearly all power structures have been thoroughly de-legitimized. Moral values have crumbled. Role models of higher ethical and spiritual attainment have disappeared. Most jobs are meaningless and dead-end. Hopelessness and fury pervade our world. Emotional maturity is not valorized as a goal of education. Marriages and families are failing at an ever-increasing rate. The media deluge us with lures of instant gratification. Cynicism has become the prevailing mode of thought, hypocrisy the dominant mode of interaction. With such attitudes, the human race cannot long hold it together.

Official acquiescence, indeed modeling, of attitudes of aggression, hypocrisy, and hatred is dehumanizing all of us. People are on edge. Anyone can crack up unexpectedly, without notice. We see it every day among celebrities. Everyone feels in danger literally all the time. Paranoia is rampant. Armed guards are being hired everywhere. But what happens when the guards themselves start to crack up? Who will protect us from our protectors? And this too is happening more and more, on every level of society. We are headed for a planetary crack-up.

What has all this to do with attaining enlightenment? A lot. In the first place, the more enlightened people we can produce, the more good energy there is to balance the bad. In the second place, enlightenment is our only hope of coping with all the madness in the world. Third, all this is happening in order to bring about the transformation of human consciousness, so by voluntarily flowing with that imperative, we are helping accomplish Nature's work of higher evolution as efficiently as possible.

We can only create a livable world again when we have restored trust among one another. And we can only do that when we fully embody the highest values of love, truth, and courage. And that requires inner transformation and spiritual illumination. This is the responsibility of each of us. We can all contribute most to world peace by bringing peace into our own souls—and into the earth of our bodies.

Will taking up meditation and doing plastic surgery on our egos bring an instant end to our frustrations and anxieties? Not likely. But the process will go a lot faster than you think—if you are fully dedicated to the work.

Moreover, there is a feedback loop between the individual and the collective. Your inner paradigm shift brings about shifts in everyone around you. Their shifts in turn support yours. It becomes a virtuous circle. And if one is part of an intentional spiritual community of mutual support for transformation, the process can really accelerate.

The stronger the links you have with such a community of people you can trust and with whom you can be authentic, the easier it is to find your inner source of strength and love. And conversely, the more one has achieved internal integration and serenity, the more support one can offer to the community. And a community that functions at a high level of spiritual awareness can skillfully support and synergize with other communities, enabling humanity as a whole eventually to awaken from the present nightmare and rise to our full potential.

The current social structures and their correlative ego structures are decomposing before our eyes. But new, healthier social structures and a more evolved humanity are simultaneously arising. Each of us must choose whether to be part of what is cracking up and dying or of what is being born and becoming whole.

Why not choose enlightenment?

Exploding Some Myths
About Enlightenment

New students on the spiritual path often ask questions based on false assumptions about the nature of reality, the point of the spiritual journey, and in particular about enlightenment. They want to know if such and such a sage was, or is, truly enlightened, if enlightened individuals still feel pain, if particular practices will bring about enlightenment, and so on. To forestall such unhelpful inquiries, it may be appropriate to clarify the nature of "enlightenment" with the following seven points:

1. Enlightenment is not an attribute of a person. It is a realization of the illusory nature of all persons, a realization that the entire universe is the dreaming of a single Self, and that the One Self is not a person, either. Enlightenment is a realization so strange, so awesome, so bizarre to the "normal" mind, so far beyond all categories of possible thought, so hilarious and delightful, that it cannot be described. No individual can possess such a realization. Rather, the realization brings the illusion of individuality to an end. (The reality of the organism, of course, is not affected. And so the organism will continue to feel pain when injured, though no ego will suffer.) As an addendum, the loss of the illusory phenomenal individuality can, paradoxically, only happen after one has fully individuated.

2. Enlightenment cannot be said to be either gradual or instantaneous. It is both and neither. It is beyond time itself. To

use a banal analogy: Does popcorn pop instantaneously or gradually? Is it not both? Doesn't there have to be a gradual heating process to produce the instant pop? Could not those who seem to attain "instant enlightenment" have been preparing for that moment for many lifetimes? Since enlightenment is not actually an attainment at all, but a realization of that which has been true forever, its apparent attainment is part of the cosmic dream. It merely turns it into a lucid dream.

3. Because the concept of enlightenment is freighted with so much baggage of misunderstanding, it is not a useful term to emphasize in serious spiritual discourse. But since every term has been contaminated by egoic misconstrual, let us accept it conditionally, so long as we recognize that it can never be the property of a phenomenal entity.

4. It would be more useful to consider spiritual unfoldment as a three stage process, consisting of Awakening, which implies a symbolic recognition of the trap that consciousness has fallen into; a second stage, called Illumination, which consists of the intoxicating revelation of the Real Self, ungraspable by language or sensation, and the beginning of the intuition of theosis, or divinization, which is the equivalent of the Buddhist concept of emptiness; and finally, the redemptive attainment of the Supreme Liberation. This refers to a state of unwavering and total detachment and dis-identification from any objective correlative to consciousness or any content of consciousness, including the most subtle visionary images, sublime feelings, and exalted conceptualizations.

5. Enlightenment has nothing to do with claims to knowledge of things in the phenomenal world. Attainment of enlightenment will not make one a great physicist nor even a competent

plumber. It does not mean one can see into the future in any specific way, nor that one has any miraculous powers. It does not even mean that one gains the appropriate temperament to be a good spiritual teacher.

6. Let us also make clear that authentic Self-realization has absolutely nothing to do with any of the following:

- channeling or receiving messages from "higher beings" or the dead;

- saving the world from the forces of darkness;

- religious piety or ritual behavior;

- taking substances to achieve altered states of consciousness;

- walking around labyrinths painted on the floor;

- surrounding oneself with crystals;

- doing "energy healings" or homeopathy, chiropractic, or other forms of medicine;

- reading Tarot cards, astrology charts, or consulting the *I Ching;*

- going into trances;

- tantric sexual activity;

- special diets;

- athletic performance, whether it be triathlons, hatha yoga, or tai-chi;

- improving one's self-esteem.

None of the above activities are being condemned. Some of them may be quite pleasant, healthy, and useful, others less so. If performed in a state of mindfulness, some of those activities can produce ecstatic experiences. Trained shamans can use such practices and the altered states produced by hallucinogenic plant substances for healing purposes. But such ecstasies have nothing to do with enlightenment. If this is not understood, they can degenerate into a form of idol worship.

7. Spiritual unfoldment, leading to the attainment of Self-realization and Liberation, does not require the assistance of an outer teacher. But because of the tenacious and deceptive nature of the ego, the help of a skilled spiritual guide and a supportive community can accelerate the process tremendously.

The Enemies of Spirit

The main enemies of spiritual progress are love, goodness, and purity. This may seem surprising, but the reality is that the ego's love is not true, its goodness is a sham, and purity is often a forced torment, a wall of denial and hypocrisy, and an excuse for narrowness and prejudice.

In Sanskrit, there are dozens of words for love. Every variety, level, and quality of love is distinguished. But in most Western languages, only one word is used to signify so many intentions that deception and self-deception have become systemic. So many different feelings can be secretly packed into that overloaded signifier "love" that miscommunication is inevitable. "I love you" may mean I want to dominate you, possess you, devour you, get lost in you, be enslaved by you, emulate you, become you, punish you, mutilate you, and even destroy you. Egoic love can be a very dangerous thing. We all know about fatal attractions.

Goodness may also hold one back on the spiritual path. It can be a cover for people pleasing, for denying one's truth, and for Self-betrayal out of fear of breaking social or religious rules intended to keep one from Self-realization. One must be careful not to make the idea of goodness into a fetish.

The concept of purity also gets distorted easily. The ego can use it as a cover for prejudice, rigidity, and a false sense of superiority. In the sexual realm, purity is often defined as complete celibacy, rather than a healthy and compassionate approach to sexual relationship. Celibacy is wonderful and liberating, if one is ready for it. But to force it upon oneself or someone else who is not ready, who has not gained sufficient psycho-spiritual maturity to recognize it for the gift that it is, or who is not called from within to live at that level of purity, will usually result in an eventual explosion of libidinal impulses that produce emotional reactions of shame and guilt, which may in turn ignite aggression, and may hurt many people. Thus, purification must begin at the level of the unconscious mind and its primary phantasy matrix, and include a conscious paradigm shift regarding one's identity, before it can truly be desired from the heart as more than a behavioral self-discipline. It must arise out of overwhelming devotion to God.

The notion of purity can be misused by social and religious institutions to serve as a mandate to people to maintain their internalized sexual conflicts in a state of repression. But libidinally repressed individuals are tormented. They do not reach their stated goals of spiritual exaltation. Thus, the priests, monks, and nuns (and, yes, even yogis) who must pretend to have transcended sexual urges are forced into hypocrisy. Impulsive illicit behavior often ensues. Scandals eventually break open. All of that, in turn, corrupts religion at its very core.

The ideal of purity can, on the other hand, camouflage a fear of entering into an intimate relationship in which one would feel too emotionally vulnerable. It can justify a failure to face the developmental challenge of attaining healthy sexuality. There are, of course, those who receive a true vocation to celibacy for valid spiritual reasons—but one must reflect long and deeply before taking such a step, and make sure one has truly psychologically matured enough to fulfill such a vow. Otherwise, at best, neurotic symptoms and acting-out will result more often than saintliness. If the life drive becomes too over-controlled too soon, the soul atrophies rather than grows.

A much better basis for spiritual transformation is constituted by the three virtues of hatred, madness, and lack of seriousness.

People who can own up to their hatred, and whose hatred is ferocious, have the best chance of attaining sainthood. Once they begin to hate their own ego, they will destroy its hold on them and transform it rapidly. Those who hate lies, hypocrisy, meanness of spirit, injustice, and hatred itself, will easily liberate themselves from such duplicitous attitudes.

To enter on the spiritual path, one must be a little mad. Without madness, as the great character Zorba the Greek was fond of saying, life is boring and empty. The spiritual adventurer must dare the unknown, and be eager to joust against the windmills of the ego with the passion of Quixote.

And finally, the spiritual warrior must avoid seriousness at all costs. One must be lighter than air, able to laugh at all adversity, to remain carefree and joyous when all around are bowing to misery, statistics, rumor, and false pretension.

The spiritual adept laughs as he witnesses those who gush how much they love people, for he sees how they love to control them. He watches merrily the many who affirm their commitment to goodness, yet who in private commit every sin. And he sighs to see those whose purity is merely a closed heart.

The real spiritual path is one of constant openness, originality, uncertainty, and nakedness. It cannot be cloaked in orthodoxy without losing its soul.

Ego Hunter

P eople enter the spiritual path because they are ego-haunted: possessed by egoic anxieties and other unbearable affects. The ego is subject to nightmares, addictions, irrational fears, insecurities, instability, and uncontrollable behavior patterns, including obsessive cleansing and protection rituals and acts of betrayal and self-betrayal. The ego is internally split. It thus inevitably suffers paralysis of will, which can show up as ambivalence, self-hatred, or suicidality.

The egoic mind is inherently confused. Its internal fractures make it unable to think clearly or understand its own feelings or those of others. It can only rarely follow through on its aims. The above describes most human beings today. But only a few seek a way out of the horror. Most prefer to numb their symptoms with superficial social engagement, gossip, vacation travel, oversleeping, workaholic evasion, television, alcohol and other chemicals, and sports, rather than get to the root of the issue.

To seek a more authentic life, which is the definition of spirituality, one must have the courage to gain self-understanding, to be willing to delve into the core of one's being and cope with the unbearable knowledge that is hidden there. Humility is also necessary. Success will depend on the ability to accept the help of a reliable and effective guide into the inner realms, to overcome the inevitable unconscious resistance.

The next hurdle comes in choosing the correct kind of help. There are many sorts of assistance one can choose from, ranging from psychiatrists who will offer officially sanctioned drugs; to shamans who may offer other, more powerful, mind-altering substances; to physical therapists of various kinds, who will try to release the effects of stress and repression from the musculature, the fascia, and the subtle energy meridians; to psychologists and counselors who offer hugs and superficial feel-good advice; to psychoanalysts who will listen for many years and tell you very little; to conventional religious advisors who will prescribe attendance at rituals, prayer, confession, and service. Any of these may be useful for part of the process. But eventually, one must go beyond all the approaches that remain within the ego, and which create dependencies on other people or on substances that function as emotional supports.

The traditional shamanic path, on the other hand, may throw one into frightening, non-ordinary realms too rapidly, and send one on inner journeys that may dumbfound or shred the ego, but that do not enable the consciousness to transcend its identifications. Shamanic neophytes tend to incorporate their narratives of psychedelic experiences into the egoic framework, and to mistake hallucinatory encounters with non-human powers and entities for Self-realization. Or else, they decompensate and fall into psychosis. The shamanic path, if it is genuine, is fraught with danger. And too often it leads to a dead end, in which one comes to believe one has seen all the wonders of the inner universe, when in fact one has not yet even crossed the threshold into the higher superconscious dimensions. On the other hand, there are many non-genuine shamans who offer only imaginary forms of inner journeying.

So long as the subconscious egoic mind remains at large, unpurified, one will be at its mercy. So long as the locus of control over one's consciousness remains in the hands of unconscious forces, one will remain enslaved to their agenda. Not even a sincere attitude of surrender to God will avail, so long as one identifies as a sinful ego, because one cannot surrender what one does not possess. The unconscious mind will not surrender without a struggle. The commitment of the conscious mind cannot be wholehearted until the unconscious ego, the superego, and the terrain of the primal phantasy matrix have been conquered. To be successful in that battle, there is no alternative: one must realize the super-conscious Self. This is the meaning of the primary metaphor of the *Bhagavad Gita*: the devoted consciousness must take the help of the True Self, there represented by the form of Krishna, to gain victory as a spiritual warrior. The Real Self alone has the power to dissolve the matrix of delusion that resides in the unconscious.

Once the phantasy matrix has been revealed, through the process of enlarging awareness—a process involving meditation, dream analysis, and the working through of emotional conflicts via transferential enactments—then one will become free of all the fixations and identifications that have held consciousness in egoic form. By completing the process of mourning, detachment, and dis-identification from all the self-images and superego voices and other mental objects that cause desire and fear, one attains the threshold of freedom. The next step is to release all sense of concreteness or illusory self-form, as well as any remaining dependence on imagery, language, and symbolic representations. When all contraction, concretization, fixation, and self-objectification have been released, the Awareness that is the Real Self, *Shunyata*, is realized as eternal liberation.

Once one commits to a serious spiritual path, and follows it with discipline—meditating regularly, processing dreams, symptoms, and other irruptions from the unconscious, studying fiercely to gain true understanding—then it will not be long before some distance from the ego can be achieved, some breathing room, some comprehension of its subtle dynamics.

Knowledge creates a modicum of power, an ability at least to observe, analyze, and contain anxieties, if not to change core patterns. But the ego will fight back. The superego complex will attack you for daring to individuate, to leave behind the imaginary matrix of unconscious phantasies for an abstract, bloodless, symbolic existence.

Fear of becoming different, of entering the unknown, fear of madness, anger at losing the right to blame others for one's lack, rage at the loss of one's comfort zone of manipulative emotional rackets, of seductive pleasures and the game of one-upmanship, of sadistic vengeance or masochistic moral superiority, and many other such temptations, can easily persuade consciousness to remain glued to its obsolete fixations. One may become even more miserable than before, because now one truly knows better. One is forced to witness one's own perversity; anguish and self-disgust mount, but one cannot fight free. One recognizes with self-loathing that one is a hopeless egoholic.

The sense of hopelessness is the essential catalyst toward authentic transformation. There is no way around what must be done: you must become an ego hunter. One must track down the ego at its root and destroy it. One must crush its destructive urges and channel its energies toward liberation. This is the all-important step of commitment to transcendence, the mark of a true Sat Yogi. One must create a space of emptiness in the mind, an ego-free zone, in which to capture the ego once and for all. For this, one must reach the first level of samadhi, called savikalpa, a very deep stage of meditation. Savikalpa samadhi refers to the ability of consciousness to lie in wait, as a hunter must do, until the ego arrives, and then crush it in the jaws of Nothingness. One must hold onto the thrashing ego and not let go until it gives up the ghost—the Holy Ghost that is seemingly trapped within, the Atman.

To do this, one must appropriate the ego's destructive energies and use them against the ego itself. The result of this effort to annihilate the false self is a new lightness of being, through which will emerge the deeper wisdom of the archetypal plane, and will lead to the subtlest energies of Pure Spirit.

The sacred work of self-conquest can only be achieved through utmost devotion, perseverance, and perspicacity. One must be willing to sacrifice one's most cherished offspring, one's inner child.

This is the moment metaphorized in the Torah as God's command to Abraham to sacrifice his son, Isaac. It is again emphasized in God's own later sacrifice of His only-begotten son, Jesus. Each of us must sacrifice the ego in a ruthless act of self-transfiguration, for the sake of truth, love, honor, freedom, and yes, for the sake of life itself. Our innocent planet, Earth, now requires this sacrifice of all of us, for the sake of Mother Nature herself. Our mother, the biosphere, is dying, as are all our relations, the world of our animal brethren, our sacred plants, life-giving rivers, living oceans, and holy mountains, all because of the pathological condition of the human ego. The sacrifice of the ego has become a bio-spiritual imperative.

The successful ego hunter kills his prey with a single blow. One should not allow the ego to die slowly in agony, but take it quickly out of its misery. One must be especially careful not to simply wound it and let it escape. There is nothing more dangerous than a wounded ego. Until one completes the sacrificial act, one's life will remain on hold. There is no time to waste.

Killing the ego is only the beginning. It creates an opening. It reveals the underlying emptiness, the absolute nothingness at the heart of one's egoic identity. One must not hesitate to enter this nothingness, to realize that nothingness IS the Real Self. One must not make the mistake of intellectualizing about this fact, or one will doom oneself to roam the hell realms as a mere philosopher. The ego will then re-manifest in a more sophisticated form, and become even more difficult to kill. One must not turn nothingness into something by objectifying it, conceptualizing it, or turning it into the theme of yet another ego narrative. One must fall freely, totally, absolutely, into the nothingness, realize that one IS nothing, and dissolve all thought in the infinite emptiness of presence without end. This is the meaning of Nirvana.

Only then will it become clear that the abyss of nothingness that is the Heart contains the whole universe—that the Universe is alive, it is the Being and Creative Source of all that is and is not. The Universe as a whole, including death and non-being, including dimensions beyond the physical, including realms of strangeness beyond imagination, including the Primal Light and Awareness, the Quantum Wave from which it all sprang, the *Spanda* of pure potentiality, is the very self-expression of the Absolute. It marks the first emanation from the inconceivable Fullness of the Godhead. In that timeless instant of recognition, Nirvana and Samsara become one.

This is the moment of union with Brahman, the realization of the Absolute as ultimate paradox, unity expressing itself as disunity, harmony as conflict, nothingness and totality as mirror polarities each supporting the other, all cascading from the fundamental self-splitting of God into Light and Awareness, phenomenon and noumenon. And beyond that apparent split, ontologically prior to the cleaving of the unitary Real into duality and multiplicity, the unity of the Transfinite, Self-Luminous Essence remains forever whole and eternally present.

The entire trans-cosmic process unfolds as spiraling Time (the moving image of eternity, the dance of space/matter/energy/consciousness), the endless play of the One-as-the-Many, while the Absolute remains forever transcendent—serene, pure, luminous, loving, and unutterably beautiful. In the pristine moment of supreme awe, liberated presence is reconciled to everything that has ever been and ever will be. Life is perfect exactly as it is.

And here we are, in the midst of this awesome process of attaining enlightenment, the supreme liberation of Spirit, while humanity is seemingly spinning out of control in the cataclysmic transfiguration from one historical age to another—in the midst of what is destined to become a great die-off of our species and most of Nature's current forms of life—on the way to a new roll of God's dice.

Control of this sublime process is impossible. We can only trust and enjoy the majesty of the greatest game of all that is underway before us and within us. Faith in the goodness, wisdom, and power of the Supreme Intelligence is the key to achieving the optimal outcome. Trust the Ground of Being. Make it your Happy Hunting Ground.

The Great Tapestry

Reality is a tapestry of infinite complexity—one that we weave, and out of which we are woven. The dual nature of our relationship to the world—we are both its creatures and co-creators—is the source of many of the most fascinating paradoxes of art and logic.

The world is our idea, as Schopenhauer observed, our projection—and at the same time, the cause of our desire and frustration. Though, indeed, we are the weavers of our world, we are mostly unconscious of that fact. We tend to recognize only half the story, to feel that we are the world's epiphenomena—or worse, its victims. Our part in the creation, and the incomparable artistry, of this grand tapestry of cosmic reality is too often denied. This is most true in moments of boredom or suffering—until some uncanny event occurs that astonishes us with its piquancy, its utter improbability, its poetic poignancy.

Such events as synchronicities and moments of déjà vu, those extraordinary moments of absurdity or poetic justice, in which we can hear God's laughter; or the simple delights of encountering a flower, drinking a cup of tea, or otherwise enjoying the perfection of a timeless instant, as when we find ourselves briefly at home again in Nature—such moments of humbling and awakening, moments of lucidity and love, of presence in eternity, in which the ego drops its shields and blinders, its linearity and alienation from the Now—force us to bow to the grandeur, the sublime majesty, and the exquisite beauty embedded in the very threads of Creation.

In order to appreciate the awesome tapestry of the Real, we must pay close attention. We must be willing to transcend our normal representational consciousness. We need to become aware of the ineffable fact that all that we perceive is consciousness itself. It is in the recognition that we live in a psychic reality—that what we take to be the external physical reality is consciousness itself—when our higher capacities begin to unfold. This is the beginning of both art and philosophy, which have always been medicine for the human soul. In fact, the soul is congealed out of this awareness of deeper and more hidden patterns and meanings in reality than those that can be formulated in material, temporal, and utilitarian modes of relating.

In the lower unconscious strata of the soul lie the dark clouds of phantasy regarding what it is to be a man or woman, the childhood complexes in which our capacity to desire and even to sense, to think, to intuit, or to feel, are locked up or forced into conflictive and tormenting double binds.

In the infernal levels of the unconscious psyche, we are indeed the woven weavers. The tapestry of our relations depicts the distance and despair, the longing and the impotence of having lost the first objects of desire, the music of love re-composed in the key of anger and impossibility.

But at some point, as it happened with Dante, we find ourselves beginning an odyssey toward inner knowledge. It often starts with an aesthetic revelation, one that functions as a kind of psychic surgery, removing some dark mass from our mind. Art, music, dance, dream—the subtle medical instruments of Aesculapius—have long been known to draw out from the soul its darkness of destructive and demeaning demand in a crystalline catharsis of emotional color and *calor* that transforms concupiscence into epiphanies of extroverted inwardness and sacred individuation.

We are led further inward by enigmas posed to us by the majesty of the tapestry of life itself. Tantalizing hints of higher truths appear in our interpersonal interactions, in archetypal dreams, in our unexpected psychosomatic reactions to events, as well as in the feelings that up-well within during moments of solitude, when we know we must follow the track of those clues clearly left for us by an unknown Other. The journey of discovery must go on until the thread of Ariadne runs out and leaves one alone in the inner labyrinth with the minotaur who rules the mind: the Censor, the author of a thousand cuts of thought-links, cuttings that keep insights unborn, a thousand ways of veiling the Real to maintain the delusions of the ego. Once this monster is destroyed, we are flooded with new information, knowledge that dissolves the walls that bound the field of meaning on which we had bet all too much of our lives.

Thus begins a phase of waiting and unweaving—as the soul becomes Penelope at night, awaiting the return of her Beloved—that weans one finally of ego fantasies. In the unweaving of our pseudo-Being, we learn to cope with loss and lack and emptiness. In the falling away of all our projections and self-representations, the dualities of thought lose their polarities in a density of pure experience that can no longer be held at a distance: One becomes the Real. No longer does one witness the tapestry from a safe distance, as in a museum, but one dissolves into the field of living energies, becomes the flowing and flowering of Chaos, an infinite excess of universes, cosmos after shimmering cosmos pouring out of Nothingness and back into Nothingness again—consciousness pouring into consciousness, God flowing from the Godhead into the Ocean of Her own transfinite depths, breathing vitality and light into Her unformed and empty essence, an incessant cascade of love, of luminous thought-forms of pure beauty, pure life, each exquisitely dying forever into the all-absorbing darkness of the Absolute.

The intrigues, the feats of petty heroism, all the tortured extimacies of the ego's charade of supposed significance, pale shamefully when contrasted with the energies that give birth to the play of life and weave the tapestry on which our pitiful crusades are fought. Beyond the endless weaving of awareness and light lies the silent source of time and space, sweetest refuge from the cruel commotion of the carousel of our divine/demonic drives.

Within yet beyond the unfinished Tapestry of Being, beyond the furthest reaches of consciousness, we dissolve the last atom of ego into the Primal Vibration that is our source. Reunited in love, we melt in this ultimate eternal moment of union with the Absolute. Ah, God! In the final gasp of rapture, the realization that everything, every instant, is in all ways affirming the perfection of the prayer that is perception, the Great Tapestry becomes complete.

PART THREE

Illumination

The Relevance of Prayer

All creativity is structured like a prayer. Even those artists, poets, scientists, and philosophers who consider themselves atheists are, when they search within for inspiration, engaged in acts of prayer.

Great ideas do not originate in the ego, but in the beyond within. When we turn our attention inward, to the Source of consciousness, curtailing the production of thoughts, we enter a profound silence. If we remain interiorized in the silent, thought-free, awakened state for long enough, we enter into the Divine Presence. In Vedic thought, this ultimate reality is often referred to as Atman. In other schools of Indian philosophy, a variety of terms are used to signify the same Real, including Purusha, Shiva, Nirvana, Shunyata, and Brahman. In the Western monotheistic philosophies, the divine state of Being is referred to by such names as Ruach Ha-Kodesh, Ayn Sof, Christ-consciousness, and in Islam, the many names that refer to the sublime attributes of Allah.

An atheistic materialist can have no adequate concept to explain the source of intelligence that is apparent in dreams (and thus must deny that dreams display such signs of intelligence) or inspirations (including scientific ones), or in Nature (and thus must succumb to the incoherent notion of random, meaningless chance as the only engine of evolution).

Creative thinking begins with the recognition of failure. The intellect realizes that it has no good answer to an important question. Neither deduction nor induction can supply a solution. The mind cannot express an understanding that lies beyond its ken.

115

Therefore, in order for humans to grow, to evolve, to transform, they must be able to reach inward to the source of truth, and have the visionary-cognitive capacity to apperceive what has never been formulated in words or symbols within that field of discourse. The source of this capacity that transcends definition corresponds to the ancient Chinese concept of the Tao. Heidegger employed the term Appropriation. The ancient Greeks spoke of humans as having *capax omnium*, the capacity to know all.

This most subtle of all desires, the urge to attain the God-Self, is the essence of prayer. It involves a reaching inward of intelligence toward the source of consciousness. It entails the opening of the inmost awareness to the vibratory energies of transcendental intuition. It leads to an understanding that surpasses all symbolic forms. In such a moment of grace, there is reception, with gratitude, of that Absolute Power and Presence who will always remain mysterious, inherently incomprehensible, yet is revealed as the Ground of Being. These steps constitute the essential elements of prayer.

Meditation is simply the penultimate phase of prayer. First, there is a search, a questioning, a seeking of deeper understanding, and recognition of the limits of the thinking mind. There follows an implicit or explicit surrender to the higher intelligence of our Supreme Innermost Being. And then there must follow a period of listening, of humble waiting, of self-transcending love for the Absolute, the source of the wisdom that is for human beings the very water of life. This is what is called meditation. Finally, meditation itself is surpassed, and one enters the state sometimes called contemplation, or in Yogic terminology, *samadhi*, when the mind attains complete silent absorption in the Self. From this Source, new insights will emerge, once the reasoning function translates the vibratory input it has thus received. When attention remains fused with the Self, long enough for ego identification to dissolve, Liberation is achieved.

Without the willingness to ask, to seek the Source, to surrender to the ultimate intelligent awareness within, spiritual growth cannot attain its highest potentials. Without the desire to know the Power that precedes any paradigm or perspective that can be formed by the mind, the ultimate realization will remain unknown. Without the urge to pray to the Source of all knowing, and to receive the Word beyond words, there can be no true creativity. There may still be cleverness and logic, association and imagination. But the ultimate potential of creative Mind will remain untapped.

Of course, such prayer need not be called prayer. Nor need it be placed in any religious context. This process transcends categorization. It does not matter that many people do not name or praise in formulaic phrases the One to whom they address their secret prayers. That One is beyond names and forms or concern with ritual. But without authentic prayer, or true communion with the One, life becomes barren, stultified, and impoverished.

Many creative people only pray for limited realizations and understandings, however. They pray in order to solve a particular problem, or to receive consolation regarding a temporal disturbance or compensation for a particular loss. The larger horizon offered by prayer—that of realization of the Absolute and liberation from suffering and illusion—is rarely alluring for those whose identity is embedded in the material plane.

Those who refuse to pray at all tend instead to complain. Such people can be very difficult to live with. The narcissistic ego can be defined as one that denies in fact (though perhaps not in lip service) the Cosmic Mind who dwells beyond the ken of the egoic mind. Such an ego dismisses prayer and falls into habits of blaming, jealousy, and envy. It fashions a generally mean-spirited personality.

Sometimes, of course, the narcissist wears a mask that makes it appear as an inverse narcissist. Such people think of themselves as unworthy of God's attention. They believe they are too abject to merit an answered prayer. They turn this negative self-image into a form of arrogance, ultimately wreaking vengeance on the world by making a mess of their own lives—and once again, blaming "loved ones" for their own failure to live creatively and joyously.

The solution is to pray—humbly, wholeheartedly, and ceaselessly. Not petitionary prayer. Not formulaic phrases entoned by rote. But the kind of prayer that sets the mind on fire. It must be a prayer of such concentrated devotion that divine sparks fly and set aflame the veils of Maya: Such a constant barrage of prayer that the entire structure of egoic sentiment and spiritual sedition is burnt to dust and ash. In that state, all of life becomes a prayer. Doing the dishes is a prayer. Reading a great book filled with wisdom is a prayer. Eating, exercising, bathing, conversing, all become acts of prayer.

But one must be unflinchingly truthful with God. You cannot fool the Supreme Intelligence. If God wants anything, it is one's nakedness, emptiness, one's utter surrender—and not some pre-scripted performance according to the Book. One must gather the courage and vulnerability to offer one's most intimate lack, one's ruptured wholeness, one's unthinkable desires, one's anguished and unspeakable sufferings, impelled by the deepest yearning for redemption, escaping from out of the unsoundable depths of one's broken heart. Offer this to the unknowable Savior within, the ultimate source and judge and hearer of all the silent cries and whispers of one's soul. Offer all that you lack until you are nothing but pure nothingness.

Real prayer produces its own answer, one that comes in the form of the silence itself. The silence grows in power, in intuitive wisdom, in love. The waiting evolves into eternal peace. That is the final significance of the act of prayerful meditation. The answer received is the Emptiness that is filled with grace. The ego dissolves, along with all its questions. There is no one left who requires any further answers.

In the ultimate moment of Truth, consciousness Realizes All. What had been prayer resolves into rapture and redemption. It can happen for you at any moment, and for all eternity. This is how saints and sages, prophets and avatars, are born, out of the prayerful death of the narcissistic ego. They suddenly realize they are no one.

And no one outgrows the need to pray.

The Yoga of Perfect Moments

Sat Yoga could well be thought of as the practice of creating perfect moments. A perfect moment is one in which you feel fully and vibrantly alive, present, open, flowing, serenely confident and composed—at one with the universe. A perfect moment is a moment of grace.

For most people, such moments are rare. When they do happen, they are usually situational—requiring an occasion such as an expensive vacation, arrival at a remote beach or mountain peak, optimal weather, and the presence of the right companion in the right mood—and often even that scenario must be augmented with alcohol or other recreational substances to take the edge off stress or other internal blocks to relaxation and ease.

A Sat Yogi is someone who knows how to enjoy perfect moments every day, all day, without having to spend money, travel to unpopulated locations, or ingest psychoactive chemicals. The measure of one's progress in Sat Yoga is how often the perfect moments come and how long such moments last; how resistant they are to interruption; and how effectively one can help others to enjoy such moments. At the most advanced level of practice, life becomes one eternal moment of perfect ecstasy—an ecstasy that is not disturbed by seemingly adverse situations.

Part of the practice of Sat Yoga is to notice when something occurs in one's consciousness that punctures the perfection of the moment. It is usually some undesired event, ranging from a minor inconvenience to major catastrophe, from physical pain to loss of a loved one, from an unkind word spoken by a friend to victimization by crime or war, or some natural disaster like an earthquake or tsunami. Some people can handle the most profound tragedies with aplomb, while others collapse into chaos if they must spend an afternoon in unpleasant company. Sat yogis learn how not to allow such events to disturb their equilibrium. This means that one must become immune to the slings and arrows that are part of most social interactions, and to develop the power to remain centered and comfortable whether in solitude or a crowd, at a gala dinner or stuck in a traffic jam. All events, no matter how apparently aversive, can still be perfect moments. This is the payoff for those who have reached the highest levels of spiritual practice.

Of course, we all know there is no free lunch. So what is the price of this ultimate hedonism? How is it achieved? Simple. One must become fully present. The more present one is, the more serene and detached one will be. The more present, the more Self-possessed and flowing one becomes. To be more aware, obviously one must be less unconscious. Therefore, a Yogi needs to engage in a process of flushing out the subconscious thoughts, affects, fantasies, and assumptions that structure the subconscious mental body. Once the subconscious strata of the mind have been purified, one's presence in the moment will not be disturbed by internal factors. Negative and destructive affects can only fester so long as the mind holds on to negative beliefs and phantasies, image-scenarios of a bad self and/or bad others.

Of course, one must constantly practice eliminating thought-constructs from the conscious mind as well. That is meditation. Most of the thoughts that flit through our minds are banal, egocentric, and oppressive (either of self or other). Once one has gained mastery over the entire mind, and prepared an inviolable space of silence and peace that is always accessible, then one is very close to the goal of living forever in the perfect moment that is eternally present.

To succeed in gaining mastery over the mind, however, you must realize who and what you are. This requires a process of cognitive self-enquiry leading to a radical dis-identification from all objectified elements that make up the false self. Once we peel away all the images and concepts that have encrusted our consciousness, we arrive at pure awareness.

Naturally, this is a process requiring dedication, since there is usually great attachment to our identifications. Only when one realizes that such fixations stand in the way of experiencing endless perfect moments—and that egoic self-images are not authentically part of the Real Self—will one let go of all mental constructs. One must release even the subtlest levels of identification—not only judgments about personal traits (and the traits themselves), but also reflexive identification with family, nation, religion, race, sexual orientation, age, and gender—and even the identification with the human species. In fact, we must realize we are not material beings at all, and dis-identify from things of all kinds, and finally even from identification as a spiritual entity.

One must reach absolute nothingness. The root of consciousness is completely empty of content, and thus objectively non-existent. Yet this nothingness is the opening in which Being arises. So in the final realization, absolute nothingness is full with all that is, in fact the two polarities of all and nothing are realized as a single paradoxical whole. This is the Supreme Self. Once this is realized, the illusory ego dissolves in the grace of the Self's transfinite Presence.

It may take a number of falls from grace before succeeding in making the realization of the truth of absolute emptiness constant, but that happens eventually. Grace is the natural state that we are all intuitively seeking, we only need to remove the barriers through intelligent effort, and once realized in its fullness, no power could convince us to drop back into the lower realms of suffering over an illusory entity.

In truth, if one has the courage to drop all self-deceptions immediately, no other effort is required to reach the ultimate state, since it is already here and now for the taking. Because the ego is false—just a mask over the inner abyss to hide our nothingness from ourselves—nothing need be done in order to reach the goal. Only accept what is obvious. You do not exist as an objective being, and therefore not as a subjective being, either. You are an absence, an aperture, an opening through which the world appears, a world that can only be the projection or manifestation of this very emptiness itself.

But that means that absolute emptiness generates three distinct primordial powers: Intelligent Awareness, Light, and Love. The world can be understood as light in its various permutations into energy, form, and mass. Light never appears except as the reciprocal of awareness. And the two are bonded by the principle of divine love. It is the vibrational field of love that gives birth to worlds, whether individual dream-worlds or entire universes.

The dream expresses the dreamer. The world expresses its Creator. This act is known in Christian theological terms as *Natura Naturans*—Nature Naturing, constantly creating new forms to reflect the sublime majesty of God, but mutating in response to the psychic emissions of humanity. Humans are the vehicles of self-awareness for the planet. Your organism is a vehicle as well as an archetypal symbol. We humans are co-creating our planetary reality. When human love is present in its pure form, our world appears as a paradise. Once our love has been repressed and distorted into hate, the world becomes a hell. The only thing to do when one finds oneself in hell is to awaken and re-dream it as heaven. It is love alone that can re-make our world into an Edenic Garden.

As is the case with a dream, you are creator, enjoyer, and, upon awakening, the destroyer of the current hell. You have the power to bring heaven once again to this planet. The best part is: it will only take a moment—one perfect moment.

The Four Pillars of Sat Yoga

The four main pillars of Sat Yoga are meditation, Self-understanding, reframing, and egoless action. Integrated practice of these four will enable one to attain durable serenity, the ability to enjoy everything that life brings, as well as a deepened capacity for perseverance, empathy, higher purpose, and general personal power.

The art of meditation consists of sitting still, silencing the mind, turning attention inward, toward its own Source. In the absence of obscuring thoughts, one can feel the presence and power of that which gives rise to, encompasses, and permeates our consciousness.

In the surrender of the surface mind to its own depths, a richer realm of psychic energies and insights becomes palpable. A feeling of profound love emerges spontaneously from within. One is eventually lifted into unexpected sublime dimensions, discovering ever more subtle frequencies of luminous energy, ever vaster love, greater coherence and universality. Consciousness in perfect stillness soon transcends the limits of egoic identity and the constraining paradigms of symbolic thought.

Nothing beyond that point can be described in words. This is the threshold of the mystical. Once beyond that threshold, the ego dissolves, at least temporarily. In any case, it will not return the same as it went. There will be a transformation in one's sense of identity and in one's life.

If meditation is practiced regularly, the ego will morph into a qualitatively different kind of entity, deserving of the word *soul*. In the deepening process of contemplation, the soul will continue to become more refined, more open, more loving, more an immaculate expression of the Supreme Being. Ultimately, the soul will melt into the One Self, the Source, until only That remains.

The deepening of meditation requires time and ripening. That can be accelerated by the work of self-understanding. Through the ongoing exploration and expression of one's Being (through such activities as the creation of art, the practice of *asanas*, movement and dance, the yoga of sound, metaphysical reading, journaling, oral free association, and dream analysis), one will discover ever more of the hidden regions of the soul. Karmic knots will loosen, and greater freedom and joy will be experienced as one's birthright. One comes to understand the conflicts that create psychosomatic symptoms, as well as the super-conscious forces behind synchronicities, visions, paranormal occurrences, and other non-ordinary events.

The practice of self-analysis and the growing comprehension of the meaning of what irrupts from the depth dimensions of our surface lives are essential facets of the process of purification of soul. This will bring about more profound surrender to the highest intelligence that is within us. Gradually, we learn to allow wisdom and love, rather than the ego, to determine all our decisions and actions.

The ability to reframe our experience according to a more coherent and multidimensional paradigm of reality is the third crucial pillar. By translating the chaotic data of our existence into a profound vision of the highest meaning, every event comes to provide an essential piece of the great puzzle of reality, leading always closer to the attainment of ultimate union with the Absolute. It is this clear and ever deepening recognition that makes life continually astonishing. We can see that our lives are mazes in which we have been set down, like guinea pigs in a laboratory, in which we are given, indirectly, the assignment of discovering the door of liberation.

Beyond that door lies eternity, truth, and ecstasy, the Supreme Real. Once we understand that we are inhabitants of a cosmic dream, and that everything that happens is non-accidental, that everything is a clue to the ultimate mystery, then, at last, we can begin to really enjoy the process. One of the clues that we receive time and again, but always seem to misread, is that our primary task is to learn to relax.

Inner serenity is essential to the solution of the great mystery of existence. This is because the false ego identity is wrapped around the trauma of insecurity. We are born helpless in a terrifying world. Our fears have caused us to build massive defenses around our heart. We live in some degree of paranoia, and create a strategy and personality system geared to overcoming what we wrongly consider our greatest dangers.

To some the danger is ridicule, of being found inferior; to others the peril is abandonment; to still others it is engulfment, being taken over by another. To some it is all the above—life itself is the danger to be avoided. For many, the danger feared most is physical violation. For others, the greater terror is going mad. For everyone, there is at least subliminally a dark cloud of anxiety, a vague fear of impending doom, of falling into an abyss of loss and lack.

The collective social system uses those fears to control its members. Few of us can ever honestly say we are in a state of complete relaxation. This is an art we must learn, on the mental as well as the muscular, even the cellular level. The unconscious mind continuously replays our most terrifying phantasies and repressed traumatic memories. The muscles and the inner organs hold our unarticulated stress. If this stress is not released, it will eventually cause failure of one or more organic systems.

Once we recognize that life is a dream, a cosmic game, with liberation as the ultimate prize, our aim can shift to winning the game. Paradoxically, to win this highest game, we must let go of the drive to win the lesser games, the false games that promote egocentricity and therefore stress and suffering.

All the lesser games are compensations, futile strategies to deny our fears, but they lead only to more fear and more ignorance. Understanding that fact leads us to recognize the importance of the fourth pillar of Sat Yoga: egoless action. In Taoism, this is called *wu-wei*, often translated as effortless action. There is no sense of 'efforting' because there is no ego involvement.

When we act without ego, spontaneously, from the heart, it means we are fully present, that we are intuitively responding to the needs of the moment, and that on a deep level, we recognize that we are one with the Whole, rather than simply a part-object in a world of separate forms and entities.

Thus emerges the vibrant perception of the Self as the unitary field of intelligence behind and within the universe. We intuit that all beings are aspects, modes, and nodes of the One Self. There is nothing to fear, nothing to lose. There is no lack in us, only fullness. When the inner light is illumined, and we can say with certainty, "I am the Self of the universe," then we are liberated from the limited ego, and our Being fills with rapturous love. At that moment, the door of liberation opens.

On the four pillars of Sat Yoga, a planetary community can be safely and harmoniously built.

Injoy: The Simplest Way

Learning to relax and enjoy is only the first step on the path to liberation. The problem is that it still requires effort. And since real enjoyment must be spontaneous, it cannot come by demand—not even one's own. This seems like another double bind. But there is a way out. It is to realize that there is no need to make any effort to enjoy, because you are already INJOY. If you understand this, you have found the shortest path there is.

Yes, this is the simplest of all possible ways to attain liberation in life. There is absolutely nothing to do. Simply "injoy!" Injoy means that your very nature, your essence, *is* joy. Joy is always already and forever within. You ARE injoy.

Injoy is an unusual word. It is at the same time noun and verb and adjective. Injoy is completely different from "enjoy." "Enjoy" is an action of someone, or a command, it requires a doing, it is a temporary situational experience, one that can be lost, and therefore can be longed for, which creates pain and suffering. In fact, all our pain and suffering comes from a longing for a lost enjoyment (kept distant by false beliefs regarding oneself and reality). But injoy is our nature, our very Being. Injoy cannot be lost (though we can certainly veil it from ourselves through repressing our awareness of it). We are always, at the core of our Being, injoy.

So the simplest path is to stop seeking to enjoy, and simply realize you are already injoy. This does not require any particular kind of meditation. One need not sit cross-legged, nor chant some mantra, nor even think about God. In fact, you will find God when you realize you are injoy, without even looking.

When injoy, then all things come of themselves. Flowers and birds singing and people dancing and delicious sensations of every sort flourish injoy. Life itself is injoy. Injoy is the essence of all things. Even the mind in the most rarified process of abstraction performs its representational acrobatics injoy. In fact, you may discover that even when reading, a text will actually read itself to you injoy. All that is Real is injoy. Even pain is injoy.

What could be simpler? Instead of suffering over the lack of some thing you want to enjoy, choose to realize your true nature— Injoy!

Injoy is another name for the Self that we seek to realize on our spiritual path. So, there is nothing to do but celebrate: Injoy!

Seven-Body Health Care

Growing numbers of people are dissatisfied with current mainstream medical care. There are good reasons. For one, most doctors have little time to spend with patients, either to explore the deeper causes of ailments or to explain clearly the different options for treatment. For another, physicians have become all too often mere purveyors of drugs—and those drugs, all too often, have proven to have side effects worse than the illness they are meant to treat.

More important even than that, modern medicine has no concept of what health is—only of illness. There is little or no attention paid to preventive treatment, nor to any factors but the gross physical ones. There is little difference between human medical practice today and veterinary practice. It is largely for these reasons that alternative health practitioners have been gaining adherents in recent years. But there is still no single approach that deals with the entirety of our being.

To understand what a truly integral, wholistic approach to health care in the future might look like—and how one can access those missing elements of treatment today—we must understand all the dimensions that constitute a human being. Ironically, ancient cultures were more attuned to our multiple dimensions than our current social milieu, which ideologically attempts to brainwash people to accept a reductive, flattened view of reality—one that blocks out or denies most of what makes us human. But a revolution against such one-dimensional thinking is underway. The ancient/restored teachings of Sat Yoga are part of this burgeoning wholistic revolution, one that is both multidimensional and integrative.

Sat Yoga teaches that we each have seven bodies, not just one. In addition to the food body (the gross physical vehicle, known in Sanskrit as *anna-maya-kosha*), there are six other bodies without organs: the *pranic*, or bioelectromagnetic body (*prana-maya-kosha*); the mental body, which includes what psychoanalysis refers to as the unconscious (*mano-maya-kosha*); the wisdom body, which includes the super-conscious (*vigyana-maya-kosha*); the bliss body, which includes the subtle light of pure awareness (*ananda-maya-kosha*); the transmigrational body (*sutratma*); and the universal body (*mahasutratma*).

When sought out for healing consultations, or when approaching self-healing, Sat Yogis focus first on the mental body, rather than the physical. This is because the vast majority of illnesses and accidents are psychosomatically caused or influenced. If there is, for example, an unconscious urge toward self-sabotage or victimization or even suicidality; or if there is a fundamental fear of life, or pervasive guilt, shame, or unconscious desire to suffer for another or take on another's symptoms, or to hurt another through making one's own body a proxy for the other—or any other unconscious complex that may be interfering with the healthy flow of living energies—then there will be effects on the physical body that will not be abated through merely physical treatment.

Stress, anxiety, and negative thinking depress the immune system, weaken the psychic field of the protective aura, collapse the psychological defenses, and acidify the bloodstream. In addition, many physical problems are the result of bad habits of food intake, addictions, and other lifestyle issues with an emotional underside that must be dealt with at the root, in order that a person can gain the undivided will to be well.

Treatment of the mental body requires, among other capacities, empathy and an ability to listen between the lines, an ability to uncover repressed traumas, to contain and detoxify projections, to understand dreams and other enigmatic expressions of the unconscious, and to intuit unspoken or unspeakable feelings. One must also be able to transmit psychological strength and courage to face what is within as well as cope with the outer challenges of life. Once the mental body has been purified and strengthened, maintaining the health of the physical organism becomes a much simpler matter.

The food body is generally best treated through exercise (including stretching as well as aerobics and strength training) and a change of diet. Today, most people eat terribly—too much caffeine, meat, sugar, and other refined carbohydrates. Most people are one of the following: obese and lethargic, underweight and prone to fatigue, or hyperactive and unable to concentrate. Many people are chronically depressed or else they suffer from emotional and metabolic bipolarity.

Our food bodies, especially the bloodstreams, have in many cases become acid, rather than alkaline—transformed into fetid biological environments in which toxic microforms can flourish. Our bodies also all carry a toxic burden from the pollution of the water, air, and earth, the pesticides and plastics in the food, and the excess poisons some of us ingest in the form of cigarettes, drugs, alcohol, and other substances. This toxic burden strains our physical body's resources for healing. If we have allowed the proper pH balance of our bodies to be lost, the consequences cannot but be grave over the long term.

Our physical bodies must maintain an alkaline balance in the blood. Once this is lost, then a severe cleansing fast should be undertaken to kill off the microforms and to make the body's inner environment alkaline again, so that unwelcome pleoform fungi, bacteria, yeast, and viruses can no longer proliferate. At the same time, such a cleanse will result in weight loss, eliminating fat cells that retain toxins, and enable the removal of toxins from the cells and bloodstream, permitting the body's healing powers to work at full strength once more.

In addition, the appropriate herbs, vitamins, minerals, amino acids and live vegetable juices will nourish the cells, improve metabolism, and help draw out poisons. Such a cleanse will often bring up further repressed affects from the mental body—in the form of hidden attachments to unhealthy patterns of living—including fear of vibrant health itself. Particularly in women, there may be a depressing feeling of being unattractive but there may also be a deeper fear of becoming physically too attractive. Or there may be a sense of guilt for living a happier life than one's parents, with values that differ from theirs. All these issues in the mental body must be resolved, or else negative effects in the organism will re-establish themselves.

The *pranic* body must also be addressed. The organic body is interwoven with an electromagnetic energy grid that enables the cells to communicate and function. *Prana* refers to this subtle energy that flows through the body. If the *prana* is blocked from flowing through the *nadis*, the subtle nerve pathways (called meridians in Chinese medicine), then the organs that do not receive this current of energy will begin to malfunction.

Acupuncture is one way to get the flow going again. The ancient Indian art of *ayurveda* also has approaches to aid in the *pranic* flow. Homeopathy can likewise be of help. In less severe cases, shiatsu or other deep massage may be sufficient. Another approach that is part of Sat Yoga is the practice of *pranayama*—a system of breathing exercises—which can break through impediments in the energetic flow, increase the *prana* as well as the oxygenation of the body, and also positively affect the pH balance. Correctly practicing yoga *asanas*, the well-known stretching postures, as well as chi gung and tai-chi, can also help open blocked *nadis* and keep the electromagnetic energy field generally strong. It is also important not to disturb the energy field, particularly the field around the brain, by using cell phones or sitting too close to cathode ray tubes in computers and television sets. Even wearing a battery-powered wristwatch can affect the flow of prana. Nor should one sleep with an electric alarm clock near one's head. These "conveniences" can in the long term prove lethal to our health, as many studies are now revealing.

The mental body should not be left out of the picture. In order to access our higher capacities, we must have our mental life and our values in good order. If our intentions are ethical, our actions fair, compassionate, and consistent, and our temperament is balanced, centered, and contained, then we can more easily gain the peace of mind required to enter into our wisdom body in our meditation practice.

Once the mental body has been cleansed, the wisdom body—the superconscious—and the heart, the seat of compassion, become the twin loci of consciousness. We may then undertake deeper voyages into our interior dimensions. In these inner journeys, we may encounter figures of myth or the collective creative imagination—archetypal figures—to guide us to understand more deeply the reasons for an illness or other impediment in life. Through accessing this innate wisdom, we can discover a greater context in which our life has more profound meaning than we had attributed to our existence.

The wisdom body opens us to the reality of vertical time, or being-time, time as depth, eternity, presence, rather than mere duration. Our culture recognizes only horizontal time. The latter kind of time is made up of infinitesimal 'nows' that cannot be accessed, so that we oscillate between future and past, living in exile from presence, and thus from true aliveness. As the heartmind and the wisdom body, operating in being-time, integrate fully with the mental body, the mind and the physical organism begin to function in a new way. Rather than remaining trapped in a circuit of words, living in a representational reality devoid of true presence, we realize a different way of knowing—a participative intuition—that opens the doors of perception to the higher realities that are immanent in our world, but unseen by most people. We learn to live free, outside of all boxes.

All this is part of *chakra*-cleansing. The *chakras* are psychic energy vortices that fuel our libidinal impulses. Once our lower-*chakra* psychic energies of aggression, sexual lust, and fearful self-contraction are transformed into the higher energies of love and detached discernment, the psychic energy, or *kundalini shakti*, will rise until we begin to perceive the blissful light body.

Then the work is to incarnate the light of pure awareness fully into the physical dimension. This is accomplished through surrender to Brahman, the ultimate source of our supernal luminosity. This will bring the highest grade of healing *shakti*, the divine energy, from the transcendental field of the Absolute to bear upon any physical illness, and to bring about the complete liberation of consciousness from egoic identification. This is an achievement that of course transcends the health of the organism.

It will lead us to discover our transmigrational body, the *sutratma*—the thread or trajectory of all our lives, past and future, the information on which is available to those who connect with the wavelength on which that information is recorded. We may discover that current life problems are the result of past karma—or even of future karma that may require the present learning of lessons that could only occur through an illness or other form of suffering.

Karma, in the form of *vasanas* (tendencies of mental activity) and *sanskaras* (root templates for our thought circuits and latent behavioral patterns and desire impulses that are located in the deepest levels of psychic sedimentation), accounts for the remaining blockages of the energies that must flow to maintain our health. The clearing of karma permits the *kundalini shakti* to rise to the highest level.

The final body is the universe itself—the *mahasutratma*. The universe is recognized as a single organism, the body of God, and therefore the body of each of us. At this level, we are all one. And the energies of the universe, the warp and woof of the loom of life, are all available to converge to enable us to heal. We can call upon the power of the sun, the earth, and all the energies of Nature, by merging the individual mind into the All/One Presence. To do this, we must attain utter emptiness, so that the universe may fill us with the power of life. Pure consciousness perceives directly that the universe and everything in it is God. We are That. From this realization, all blessings flow.

If we work on all seven bodies, healing can be not only effective on the physical plane, but will lead to spiritual realization and liberation, which is the real point of why we are here in the first place. It is the real reason, or final cause, behind most illnesses. We are all being led, unwittingly in many cases, to the attainment of God-realization.

But we must remember that healing is not the same as curing. Because the universe is our body, the changing of one physical body for another is not very important in the scheme of things. Let us not be afraid to drop the body when we have attained our ultimate purpose here. And let us not lose a moment in attaining that purpose. When we do that, we heal not only our individual being, we heal the world as a whole. This is the real aim of Sat Yoga.

PART FOUR

Overcoming the Obstacles

How to Get Out of a Double Bind

The ego's unconscious intentional structure has the logical form of a double bind. That means it is self-impeding. It creates mirages that it mistakes for reality, entrapping itself in an endless loop. The ego can be thought of as a complex bio-computer program with a built-in bug—or strange loop—that is responsible for the feeling that spiritual liberation is impossible.

The subliminal double-binding program remains throughout life the governing modality of the inner censor. The censor is the ruling agency of the ego. It functions as a mediator between the conscious identity and the repressed infantile self-system, manipulating the interpretation of reality. The censor enforces its agenda (of seeking the lost object of desire of infancy through projection and repetition of futile patterns and demands) through the activation of hostile/seductive superego voices and the deployment of a barrage of sophisticated defense mechanisms that keep the consciousness split, confused, and working against its own real interests.

The double bind can be most easily understood in its original form as a way of coping with the impossible tension between healthy urges for separation versus fear-based symbiosis with the mother. The child loses, no matter which alternative is chosen. If it really separates from mother, the result is anxiety: the terror of facing a vast, alien world in a condition of helplessness. If it chooses to cling incestuously to the mother, it loses its independence; it betrays its own desire for autonomy, and its spirit is thereby broken. The ego thus fears both loss of selfhood and freedom. Thus, the censor finds a compromise, choosing self-sabotage to maintain the stasis, creating indecision and paralysis. From then on, self-hatred festers. Not being able to commit to either unbearable alternative, the ego remains caught in the double bind.

The bind evolves as the child grows into adulthood, according to the vicissitudes of the environment and the soul's *sanskaras,* the qualities carried forward from previous lives. There are thus as many variations of the bind structure as there are egos. Let us examine a few of the more common ones. We can classify them into withdrawal binds, aggression binds, superiority/inferiority binds, and authenticity/bullshit binds.

Here is the history of a well-known aggression bind: A woman who, as a young girl, was chronically angry with pathologically inept parents who did not listen to her or understand her needs. Either she had to throw tantrums to get attention, in which case she was punished, or she became passive and fell into despair. Years later, she romantically connects only with men who cannot be there for her in the way she needs, and she is constantly faced with the choice of either being enraged or giving up and feeling abused. She defines love as either the sacrifice of her autonomy or the futile commitment to an endless struggle. Thus, her only heart connection with her partner is with his own traumatized and furious 'inner child', with whom she colludes in a repetitive mutual re-traumatization-revenge-and-forgiveness ritual. Her relationships are doomed to be the serial futile pairings of hungry ghosts on a rampage—unless she finds a way to escape the double bind.

Then there is the man who as a child found he got better care when he acted helpless and withdrawn. So now, whenever he takes the initiative and acts powerfully in the world, he feels abandonment anxiety. If he withdraws, he feels protected, though he is actually undermining his position in the world. If he comes out strong, he feels too vulnerable, and soon collapses in abandonment anxiety, and finds a way to justify retreating into his cave. He learns that the easiest way to justify his collapse is to frame it as a physical illness. So he learns to produce psychosomatic symptoms in his body whenever he feels anxiety. His withdrawal double bind keeps him from confidently building a successful life.

Then there are the many varieties of sexual aggression binds. In the most common, a woman does everything possible to be found irresistible by a man, but then hates him for treating her as an object. The man usually reciprocates by losing interest in her the minute he defines her as having been conquered. When she pulls away and threatens to leave, she suddenly becomes irresistible to him again.

In these cases, others who are potential sexual partners have value only to the extent they have not been captured—or to the extent they can be used as part of the larger game of social climbing. Often, the partner is desired precisely for what makes him undesirable—to ensure that one remains in control and unafraid of rejection, and to have a scapegoat on whom to project one's shadow. Being caught in such a relationship bind can use up all one's emotional energies, so that one never has to face the deeper issue of being clueless regarding one's real Self. One's thoughts are a whirlwind circling around a false self-representation caught in an endless loop scenario.

The double bind structure precipitates the activation of superego voices—usually including an obscene, seductive voice and a severe hyper-purist judge. Once those voices are in place, they function as the instruments of a second layer of psychic binding. The voices make conflicting demands both to 'enjoy' and to 'be good'. If the first of these voices is obeyed, then one is stung by guilt for failing to obey the other. Or one gives in either sequentially or simultaneously to both voices, enacting a complex submission/transgression pattern, and feels torn apart, enslaved, unsatisfied, enraged, chaotic, and impotent. Consciousness becomes filled with self-loathing. The judgmental voice, with its impossible demands, keeps one feeling like a miserable sinner, while the seductive voice offers the thrill of transgression. The otherwise powerless ego enjoys the delicious, though short-lived, feeling of power that comes with sticking it to one voice, while submitting to the other; and then reversing the process. Enjoyment at one level is torment at the other. But this is a price the ego is willing to pay.

The real price of this exhausting game is the waste of precious life. The bad karma eventually leads to collapse, possibly to suicide. In the effort to stabilize, the ego inflicts more punishment on itself. It could be isolation or self-flagellation of some kind, or austere regimes of self-improvement.

Suicidal ideation can also be warded off through the induction of lesser grades of psychosomatic suffering. Migraines are a common example. With this maneuver, the double bind is changed into a double enjoyment. The physical symptom justifies antisocial behavior, like missing work or some other (perhaps sexual) obligation. So the demonic voice scores a point. The hyper-ethical superego also scores, as it enjoys punishing the poor ego by inflicting pain upon it. Meanwhile, the demonic voice is pacified with the taking of medicines that make the ego high, effects that otherwise would be illicit and would not be allowed by the ethical superego—thus, the ego scores a point against that voice, too. In other words, everyone wins—but only because all sides lose. Such are the complicated intermeshing gears of the wheel of karma on which the ego is bound.

Probably the saddest case is the double bind of the idealistic person. One whose self-image is spiritual and loving has a problem. To protect that image, she cannot afford to do deep inner work, since the process would uncover the unbearable feelings of lack and negativity, including hatred and guilt. The image of the 'beautiful soul' would crack open—and reveal the deeper abject self-images against which she is defending. And beneath that, she would perceive a yawning abyss. People in that quandary generally seek only a diluted, airbrushed, pop version of the spiritual quest, not the anxiety-provoking blood-and-guts dark-night-of-the-soul version that is required for liberation.

On the other hand, there are people who manipulatively adopt the spiritual journey as a way to evade responsibility for important life tasks. They avoid work and family obligations by claiming their time must go to the higher work of meditation. Yet they avoid real commitment to the spiritual path by claiming they are too fatigued.

In other cases, serving family members takes away the time that could have gone toward meditation and spiritual development. Something always gets in the way. Thus, they neither attend properly to their horizontal dharma of work and family, because it is done grudgingly and without love, nor to their vertical dharma of spiritual liberation. Instead, they usually spend their free time sleeping, daydreaming, watching movies, over-eating, or indulging the ego in other ways. They believe they can fool other people, including their spiritual guide, if they have one, with their martyr narratives, but they are caught in a bind in which they are the only ones being fooled.

The jackpot question, of course, is how to escape the double bind. This has been a focus of the research into transformational psycho-technology that Yogic scientists have been pursuing for centuries. Some of their research has of necessity remained secret (because it cannot be put into ordinary language, but must be transmitted directly, energetically, by teacher to disciple). But most of it is an open secret. It can be said simply, but the words are not usually understood, at least not by those whose internal censor is still operating.

The simplest formula that can undo the bind is to realize that the Self is neither the body nor the mind. Therefore, you are nothing that can be bound. Sit in silence until the binds drop away and realize you are free. Of course, this method works only with very ripe souls. Other techniques are employed for those who are still too enmeshed in the ego identity to let go so easily. Some techniques use confusion and frustration. For example, one approach to undoing a double bind is to create a countervailing double bind. One can see this at work in the Zen tradition in the use of a *koan*, such as: "What is the essence of Zen? If you speak, you'll be hit thirty times. If you stay silent, you'll be hit thirty times!"

In many schools of psychotherapy, the intention is likewise to create a therapeutic double bind. For example, having accepted a therapist as an expert in achieving transformation, one's resistance becomes clear even to oneself as being pathological. So if one accepts the therapist, one must inevitably open to one's real being. If one resists the therapist, one is implicitly admitting the need for more therapy. Therefore, the only effective strategy to avoid self-transformation is to de-legitimize the therapist. Of course, it only takes a little distortion by projection, a little provocation, and a little collusion with friends or family to accomplish that maneuver, and voila, one is liberated from the healthy bind of therapy. Unfortunately, the prior pathological bind remains.

Religious double binds are more sturdy than therapeutic ones, but usually less helpful. In other words, if you adopt a typical monotheistic religion, it means you affirm that you are one of the chosen. Thus, one side of the bind gets clamped on. But although you have been chosen, you are still a sinner. Thus, the other side of the bind clicks shut. Now, as a sinner, you long for redemption, for mystic union with God. But if you claim to be one with God, you are a heretic, and therefore an even worse sinner. Thus, you must continue to long for God, but you must never reach Him.

A more fundamental double bind is inherent to any spiritual quest. The ego-mind longs for liberation from its sense of lack, but is weighed down by the fear of an inauthentic 'Self-realization', in which one fools oneself into believing that one has attained enlightenment when it is but a grand illusion.

This is a profound question, because we all know of gurus who thought they were a lot further along than they really were. And indeed, it is true that any appropriation by the ego of a sense of enlightenment is false and misleading. However, it is also true that the real I is not the ego. When the I is represented in language, it becomes false, because in ordinary speech it signifies the bodily speaker, rather than bodiless, transpersonal awareness. The real Self dwells always beyond thought and speech. Any use of language that proclaims 'I am the Light' will automatically be perceived by others to be a claim that the ego is declaring itself divine.

But we must not throw out the baby (the Self) with the dirty bathwater of egoic inflation. It is a valid inner realization that 'I the Self (or the Void, or the Light, or Buddha-nature) am not the ego'. But the expression of that realization in words must be transcended. Awareness must remain in the Real to which the words are pointing. When awareness traverses the *thought* of the Light and merges into the *presence* of the Light, the ego dissolves. Afterward, when transactions resume in the world of apparent duality, illumined consciousness recognizes that 'others' will still mistake it for the body-mind, and so an ego is maintained as an obligatory illusion and allowed to humbly take up its duties again, but de-cathected of libidinal energy. And all the while, the Self remains as silent, laughing, loving Presence.

This, then, is the key to escaping the double bind. Eliminate egoic identification, and there is nothing that can be bound. Consciousness can begin by realizing its nature is simply difference from its contents. No matter what consciousness is aware of—a face in the mirror, words in the mind, memories, fantasies, bodily activities, affects—consciousness remains beyond any of its contents. Consciousness is nothing in itself, absolutely nothing, only pure awareness. And the primary content of consciousness is a sequence of ego-identifications that flow within the awareness as exemplars of a limitless range of potentialities, rather than constituting an entity of some kind.

There is no entity called "I," only a variety of partial self-representations and affects that appear and disappear, located on a spectrum from the darkest and most negative to the most luminous, blissful, and boundless. Once both 'self' and 'other' have been liberated from objectification, negative emotions based on power struggles, rejection scenarios, and relations of superiority/inferiority will dissolve. In the ensuing flow of love, creative intelligence will spontaneously surge in an ecstatic stream of benevolent intentionality. In that mode, all problems resolve.

Once the vital energy of Life is freed from the muck of egoic desire—and from the short circuit caused by the pull of contradictory inner voices—consciousness regains its natural bio-luminosity. We get our halo back.

When the double binds have been removed, awareness realizes its true nature. The consciousness you are is emptiness. Emptiness reveals itself as a world of luminous forms. The Self is playing hide-and-seek. Concealment yields to Self-revelation. No separate egos ever existed.

So that is how to get out of a double bind. Realize that there was never anyone to get caught in the first place, and therefore no one needs to be liberated.

If 'you' don't yet realize this, have no fear. At some moment, emptiness will come, like a thief in the night, dissolving the illusion of separate existence. 'Your' destiny will be revealed as unbound, boundless Rapture.

The Great Indecision Scandal

A scandal haunts the world, a fact that no one dares talk about. It has far greater repercussions than all the political scandals that are revealed every day. The disgraceful truth about the human condition concerns an incapacity we hate to admit: Humans cannot make decisions. Our vaunted free will is a sham. Our ideas are a bluff. We have no clue what to do with our lives. We have no power to navigate reality. In the most important matters, we have no ability to authentically, effectively, and wholeheartedly make wise decisions. Despite the arrogance of our self-imputed power, behind the façade, we feel altogether pitiful. The collective result of this is an inability of our societies to change direction to prevent imminent mass suicide of the species.

Nonsense, you may reply. Why, we make decisions all the time. That is true. But let us candidly take a moment and analyze the decisions we have made in our own lives, those we witness in others, and the decisions that are taken by governments and corporations.

If we are honest, we will admit several points. First, most of us experience great anguish when having to take decisions. Second, when we do, we generally make bad decisions, particularly in our personal lives. Third, most of us cannot even keep the decisions we have made. Some oscillate incessantly. They go back and forth in their minds so rapidly they cannot even maintain the pretense of a commitment. Some persuade themselves that they are certain on one day, but then someone makes a negative comment, and suddenly they are off in the opposite direction at full gallop, equally as convinced of their new course as they were moments before of their old one.

Some of us do work out our decisions rationally, of course, and then we adhere to some of those decisions, and we create elaborate narratives to justify our course of action. But despite the rational façade, the decisions were actually impelled not by our cognizing adult mind, but by some mysterious power within us that manifested an impulse to act. Our conscious minds can only rationalize those energies after the fact. We are lived by our unconscious. It was Freud's uncovering of this unknown actor behind the scenes that scandalized the field of modern psychology, which has still not fully recovered. In fact, now we know that there is more than one actor lurking in the shadows—including the anxious infantile ego, both stern and seductive superego voices, archetypal forces, and the trans-rational energies of the Atman.

But wait. Some of us make mature decisions and then stick to those decisions quite resolutely. Yes, of course, there are a few people who have refined their egos to such an extent that they can function in a state of sublimated consciousness. Whether they know it or not, their minds are engaged in a form of prayer, of surrender to their higher intelligence. But most of those who seem to be firm decision-makers are actually just rigid wishful thinkers. Counterbalancing the flighty, changeable types, who cannot come to a decision, is this opposite sort, those who never change their minds, not even after their decisions have been clearly proven wrong. Such bullheaded egos are often chosen to head governments and corporations. They make a show of having iron will, but it is without intelligence. Such willfulness is not genuine decision-making, but the ridiculous acting-out of an immature omnipotent fantasy of omniscience that refuses to consider the demands of reality.

Are we not constantly astounded at the incompetence we witness in high places? And do we not see that the larger the organization, the more stupid the decisions that are taken? Large corporations, empires, complex human systems of all kinds seem to lose their grasp, their intelligence, at a certain point in their development—when they get large enough to dare to reveal the grandiosity of the corporate ego's shameless arrogance. Then all decision-making capacities are lost forever. This, in fact, is why empires fall.

In sum, there are people who cannot come to a decision, out of insecurity, lack, and loss of centeredness, and others who must stick to a predetermined course of action, but have no flexibility to adapt to changing circumstances. In either case, there is no capacity for decision-making in the true sense. One who is able to make wise decisions and follow through on them, and flexible enough to change course when situations dictate, is a rarity. A great part of spiritual development is the mastery of the lost royal art of the decision.

Ironically, the contemporary ego is far more involved in making choices than people were in times past. We learn to make choices from a very young age, before we are able to decide rationally, what food we want to order at the restaurant, what flavor toothpaste we want to use, what TV channel we want to watch, and other consumer options. But these choices are made at an emotional level, based on the primitive pleasure principle. They are not exercises in higher rationality. And at the other extreme, we are trained to make our rational decisions by blocking out our feelings. The result is that our reason is cut off from the intelligence of the heart.

At the same time, we learn through socially-embedded ideological messages that it is not in our jurisdiction to make decisions regarding the kind of world we want to live in, the values we wish to live by, the kind of character we want to develop. All that is strictly up to the establishment—exemplified by church, state, and mass media—or else determined by family tradition or peer pressure. It is even frowned upon in many circles to be too curious about alternative ways of living and thinking. Despite the success of the Western intellectual effort to break away from the ideological grip of the Church that flowered in the eighteenth century as the so-called Enlightenment, we are still controlled by a tendency toward orthodoxy. There is a desire within the ego to be boxed into a matrix determined by the Other. The matrix of our reality is accepted as a given, rather than recognized as a product of consciousness that can be altered by more fully developing the potentials of our consciousness. We do not want to know the artificial nature of what we call reality, nor of our power to change it.

We are told we must decide what to be when we grow up, but we are never informed of what it really means to be a grown-up, nor how to mature psychologically and spiritually, so that our life decisions can bear some relationship to a higher meaning than mere opportunism. It is arguable that overall we are thus less capable of making decisions today than in previous eras, in which such higher values were still palpably recognized.

To overcome the incapacity to make decisions, people go to exotic lengths. Some, as in the ancient world, still consult oracles. They may throw *I-Ching* tokens (or just flip a coin for 'yes' or 'no') or lay out Tarot cards, play muscle-testing (kinesiology) interrogation games, or see which way a pendulum swings. Or they may look for secret signs left for them by the Universe—a feather found on the street, a random headline in the newspaper, some words overheard spoken by strangers, synchronicities interpreted as interpellations by some Higher Intelligence. Or they may ask the opinions of friends, family elders, therapists, business consultants, astrologers, futurists, or other dubious authorities. But none of these methods is satisfactory. People are always left in doubt, they second-guess every answer, and their minds can never rest.

The human incapacity to make decisions has been systematically hidden from us. In order to accomplish this, social systems have historically been created in which it is simply assumed, in fact mandated, that others will make the decisions for us. In the context of ancient India, for example, the caste system operated as a decision-making matrix. The Brahmins (the priesthood) made the fundamental value decisions for the Kshatriyas (the nobility), while the Kshatriyas laid down the rules for the Vaishyas (the merchant class), and the Vaishyas gave the orders to the Shudras (the manual laborers). The Brahmins, of course, were surrendered to God— who made the ultimate decisions. Once that system became corrupted, however, the whole chain of command collapsed. The stage was set for heterodox reformations and attendant civil unrest.

But top-down religio-centric authority systems lasted for many centuries in many cultures, for example, in the form of the feudal system in Europe and elsewhere. The churchmen crowned and advised the royalty. The royalty made the decisions for the common people. Husbands made decisions for their wives. Parents made the decisions regarding what their children would do with their lives and whom they would marry. Disobedience and divorce were not options.

In medieval Europe, the feudal hierarchies came into increasing conflict with the Church, which was eventually riven by the Protestant Reformation. Rabbis, for centuries, made the decisions among the Jews, in accord with the precedents of the Talmud—but with the opening of the ghettoes, secular ideas de-legitimized that structure. In the Islamic world, the mullahs and caliphs made the decisions, according to the Sharia law—but there, too, internal schisms, colonialism, and the winds of cultural and commercial globalization eventually broke the system.

Establishing decision-making principles and practices was a major purpose of religious institutions. Then, as those institutions lost their legitimacy, the baton gradually passed. The elders of extended clans then made the decisions. Later, when the clans also disintegrated, it came down to the heads of nuclear families. Now the institution of the family has been shattered, and the other established hierarchies have been tainted as sources of wise counsel. Science is sometimes invoked as a basis for decision-making today, but scientific theories are changing too rapidly to depend on. One cannot even determine a healthy diet on scientific grounds. Ten doctors and scientific nutritionists will offer ten widely differing opinions. We are all on our own. Today, there is no rock on which to found one's life decisions. The ground is shaking beneath our feet.

Now that all our traditional paradigms and social scaffolding have been removed, we do not have shared criteria by which to make collective decisions. Not only have the collective criteria lost their legitimacy and validity. Because of pervasive cynicism and nihilism, even the personal self has lost validity. So almost no one can make a commitment to any ideal, cause, or other person. What substitutes for commitment in most cases is either apathetic passivity or hostile dependency.

Societies depend for their survival on three functional capacities: the ability of their members to sustain trust in the promises of others; the capacity of their fellows to make wise decisions in carrying out their responsibilities; and the durability and constancy of their ongoing performance. This is the essence of social capital.

The social system today maintains itself only on the basis of intimidation, and because it has created a single criterion for all decisions: monetary profit. That is the purpose of capitalism. It makes all our decisions for us. We do what we do on the basis of what is going to bring us the largest return on our investment, measured in strictly financial terms. On the individual level, that is how we decide what we will study at the university, whom we will marry, where we will live, and so on. On the national level, that is how the elite determine foreign policy. On the social level, it is the principle that determines industrial policy.

Unfortunately, such a criterion is utterly inadequate. It ignores all higher values, all ethical, aesthetic, and spiritual considerations, even biological imperatives, including our own long-term survival. The system is destroying us. But we cannot decide to change it. We have no will with which to oppose the system. We cannot make a decision even to save our planet. Is it not scandalous? Or is there a more encompassing perspective from which to view this phenomenon?

If we are to discover a more profound meaning in all this, we must understand why the ego is such a failure when it comes to taking decisions. By definition, the ego is a false self, and therefore operates from a false paradigm of reality. Of course, some egos are more false than others. It depends on how much repression is in effect, what sort of defense mechanisms are operating, how much denial one is in, how narcissistic and psychopathic is the ego structure, and similar related factors, including, most importantly, how cut off one is from the real Self, that is, from God, the creative intelligence of Nature. The more pathology is present, the less able one is to make good decisions or to honor commitments and maintain internal and external consistency.

Ultimately, every ego lacks a true center. The center of our Being lies beyond the ego. That higher center is the source of clarity, wisdom, will power, creativity, love, and serenity. Until we transcend ego consciousness, we cannot gain the power of wise decision-making. Wise decisions are expressions of the Self. They occur when, paradoxically, we do not feel that it is we who are making the decisions. Instead, we are flowing spontaneously as vehicles of the divine Presence. We as egos do not make decisions, but the One Supreme Intelligence makes them through our body-mind, once that has been surrendered to the will of the Absolute. We then enter a state of trans-decisive living.

The only decision necessary, therefore, is the decision to surrender to God. And even that decision is not really taken by the ego. But a moment comes when one realizes it has been decided. Once the ego is absorbed in God's presence, all else follows magically and life becomes a celebration of the miraculous.

However, to accelerate getting to such a point, it is useful to take vows of self-discipline. A vow is a commitment that must not be broken. This is the way it was done by the ancient yogis. Unfortunately, these days, few people are capable of keeping a vow. That is why twelve-step groups developed the motto, 'one day at a time'. That is also why they recommend that people come to a meeting every day, to reinforce the commitment to stop the intake of alcohol (or whatever other addiction is involved). The commitment to come to the meeting thus becomes the pivot for rebuilding the integrity of the damaged ego-system. Even that is often too much for people.

A healthy spiritual community operates in a similar way (although without the self-distrusting dogma of twelve-step groups that assumes one will always remain a latent addict), offering group meditations, discussion circles, and new and deeper teachings on a regular basis to sustain the momentum of transformation and the ability of the members to function consistently from their true center. In addition, an ongoing schedule of individual meetings with a spiritual teacher to confront the ego, to encourage the emergence of the Real Self, to clarify issues, dreams, life confusions, and to infuse students with energy, courage, and Self-trust, are essential ingredients to attain the goal of authentic trans-decisive existence.

Mastering the art of decision requires transfiguration. We must harmoniously braid the powers of will, knowledge, and action. To truly decide our path in life, we must cut off the greedy, conflicted, and ignorant ego. The word 'de-cide' means exactly that: to cut off.

Only when our knowledge is freed from unconscious egoic agendas and we have become receptacles of noumenal truth; when our will is no longer split, paralyzed, and dissipated; and when our skill in action has been refined through disciplined practice; in short, when we have committed our lives to the service of God, then will the grace of trans-decisive rapture descend and flow through every thought and gesture.

The fundamental realization that must dawn is that fulfillment is not to be found in the shadow world of phenomenal forms—whether in the petty pornographic pleasures of sexual possession, the power plays in the arena of politics and finance, the pseudo-security of family enmeshment, the short-term bliss of drugs and pseudo-spiritual revelry, the futile fusion with incestuous projections, or the plodding purgatory of pointless submission to the social dharma—but rather, our salvation lies in the return to the Self.

The remembrance of God, meaning the state of Absolute Emptiness, is the only exit from the hell of the disintegrating bardo of the fallen ego. Our collective passion for the forgetfulness of our true Being has led to the demise of our planet that was once a paradise, through neglect, greed, aggression, and all the other predilections of our pathological narcissism. The only way out now is to take responsibility for our sins, to auto-dissolve the poisonous ego that we have produced, and surrender ourselves to the Supreme Authority.

Once we realize our true relationship to the One Self, the ego mind will dissolve into the oceanic infinity of pure loving intelligence, and thence will ensue the ultimate rapture of divine Beatitude. It is in this return to our original essence that the world as a whole is revealed as a manifestation of the Absolute. Then all our actions will become spontaneous gestures of grace. There will no longer be any decisions to make. The God-Self is the one Decider.

At some point, you will find yourself on such a path, perhaps even without having decided to do so. That which is in you that is greater than your ego has already made the decision. It may seem scandalous, but it is already time to celebrate.

The Power of Puernography

The ego's notorious will to power can also be thought of as a will to *puer*. *Puer* is Latin for youth. The collective ego today mesmerizes itself with what Carl Jung called the *puer aeternus* complex. We are witnessing (or captured by) an obsession with juvenility and the vital energy that youth signifies—without the recognition that what the dark side of the *puer* complex entails is psychological immaturity and fear of life. What was once thought of as a passing phase, the midlife crisis, is now a chronic miasma that begins while people are still teenagers and lasts into old age. It is a symptom of a spreading psycho-spiritual stunting and petrifaction, and the only cure is to discover within oneself the true source of eternal life.

The ego, of course, looks in all the wrong places to find the magical object that will bring it to risk growth again—and life, in its fullest sense. Pornography is one of those places that men, in particular, are drawn almost helplessly, magnetically, vampirically—to suck up visually the secret, forbidden sight that will make them youthful, potent, whole, satisfied—until the image fades and another, and then another, must be viewed. The vain hope is that the next image will be the one, the perfect form, the ultimate beauty, the full revelation of the feminine mystery, the offering of full satisfaction, the one true object of fulfillment of one's lust that will at last quench all desire, and bring one peace. But like every other form of puer-nography, the photos of naked youthful bodies prove to be a mirage. The pornographic gaze has no power to devour and digest the essence of beauty, let alone the secret of life.

It is the same mirage that beckons to the gambler, whose object is the more ethereal Lady Luck. But she too cannot be conquered.

Women have their own forms of puer-nography, of course. Photos are less often resorted to—a mirror works better. The feminine narcissistic position is to *be* the ultimate object. She is in search of the male (and even more, but more secretly, the female) gaze of desire that fills her with power and satisfaction. But above all is the pleasure of mirror-gazing she master-baits herself with. And, of course, she feels the (sometimes disdained) urge to be physically filled, phallically fueled, the vaginal hole made whole, bestowed with the virile power, the magic wand, she may imagine she lacks—or that she may imagine she has. In either case, she must seem to *be* 'it' in order to *get it*. But what she gets is never IT. And so she takes ever-greater pains to keep it coming. She cannot afford to get old, to lose her charm, to see the male gaze going elsewhere. Some current forms of feminine puer-nography are more extreme than many male varieties, involving a wide array of surgical procedures to keep her body youthful and erect, to maintain the charade that her body IS the phallus.

Of course, the male and female versions of puer-nography may be adopted equally by both genders. There may even be an added thrill to take the position of the Other sex. But all these efforts to get a charge from seeing and being seen—the basic social activity, now commercialized and hyper-sexualized—eat away at the capacity for deeper relationship with Self and with the Other as authentic Being. Being, of course, cannot be seen. The Self is invisible, formless. And as it is said: out of sight, out of mind. Thus, humans have gone completely out of their minds.

Life every day becomes increasingly superficial, meaningless, and anxious. The puernographic urge arises in a poor-no-gratified ego that experiences a hunger for what it does not understand, and out of frustration projects its hunger onto what it can sensually grasp. The ego thus 'mistakes' the body (its own and the other, its own as the Other) for the Self it lacks, and that it is really, but unknowingly, seeking.

And all the while that the ego ogles and enacts the ongoing striptease that modern life has become, the real striptease is language itself—the seductive dance of symbolic thought that both veils and reveals at the same time, offering false glimpses of Being from the onrushing train of consciousness, the smoking *loco* motive to become: to be yet not to be, that is the thrill and the problem. The symbolic is the pole of meaning, but its pole dance can never reveal Being. Being is transcendent of all thought.

Puerno-graphics is no solution. But the ego itself is a graph of signifiers, and every signifier is only a representation, an abject ab-sense of Being. Beyond the façade of images, the ego is a mesh of words, and words finally signify only the lack of Being.

The male ego that gets its hard-on from gazing at the naked flesh of the undulating woman, from peering into the darkness of a vaginal canal for what can never be discovered, is one-pointedly focusing on only one thing: the thing that is not there, represented by the thing that is missing between her thighs, the lack that can finally, with certainty, be projected upon the Other, thus liberating the 'me' momentarily from its own disgusting castration, and enabling it to feel a momentary rush of fullness.

The male gaze seeks a hard-on of the heart that can only be maintained through an attitude of sadistic superiority over the very object that now carries the meaning of the missing Self. The ego's mass-perturbation becomes its (un)holy massiveness, as he transmutes the whore before him once more—unconsciously, of course—into the forlorn virgin in the manger, giving birth to a Christ who will not be his. Allah-luya, he ejaculates, the coming is his lord. The electric instant of the orgasm fades quickly into utter loss. In the aftermath, there is no peace, only the impotence of detumescence, followed by a sadness soon suppressed by sleep or further disingenuflections leading to the same finality. Every john is just another Joseph. And every Christ is merely grist for the mill of crucifixion.

Sex is the religion of the ego. Sex leaves it attached to, yet oddly disconnected from, the Other, lost in its own lack that widens further the gap between itself and its erstwhile object of desire, desire that soon mutates into scorn, envy, fear, disgust, and hatred—shared emotions that nearly every married couple know. The ego then seeks its salvation through works, evading the withering gaze of the abjected spouse who has become the carrier of the ego's own lack (and thus remains both judge and virgin mother of the unknown Self) through economic productivity, thereby gaining a sense of selfhood by supporting a spawn of ingrates. Nearly every family in our degraded culture is built around a lack of love. And the urge to puernographic pursuits is the only covenant they hold in common.

Eventually, the ego that addictively seeks its Being, its power and wholeness, through the sexual conquest of the Other, either in the mirror, the flesh, the photo or the fantasy, finds itself enfeebled, empty, pitiful. Every conquest is eventually lost, because no deeper, lasting relationship can be built on that basis.

Women have the option of puernographic pregnancy, of course. It is one way to be filled by the Phallus that lasts. But eventually most children psychologically separate from the mother, and the old state of castration returns with a vengeance.

The will to remain a *puer* is finally an urge to self-deception. It is not only about youthful potency and sexual mastery, but about lubricating two infantile unconscious phantasies at once: that of oneness with the Mother and that of usurping the symbolic place of the Father. (The figures are reversed at another level of the fantasy, but the result is the same.) The act of sex is thus also an act of murder, as Freud discovered. But as one usurps the place of the murdered Father, one is in turn murdered—the ego murders the Self—and then buries itself alive (through repression) as

162

punishment for its crime. The ego is thus hatched out of the very plot in which its Self is then buried.

The oedipal plot is an old one, but these days it is never resolved. People do not work their way out of it, because there are no longer effective rites of passage. Thus, the ego remains forever burdened by the ancient guilt that is its original sin, a forbidden desire that propels it to its Fall, and that constitutes its ongoing futile revolt. It is doomed to struggle ceaselessly against superego delusions, rather than seek its lost Self, the only power that can liberate it from its suffering. Only the peace of the Self, that passeth the understanding of the ego, can slay the wrathful deity of guilt that haunts the ego's nightmares.

Entombed by its own repressed unconscious, the ego, acting as warden and censor of its own denied desires, forgets that all the fantasies that fill its weary days and nights, are puernographic delusions. It is all a tempest in a teacup. And while chasing its own tale, its pseudo-remembrances of times past, it loses the opportunity for authentic presencing. And so the ego lives in proustian limbo, and no amount of procrustean parsing, neither fasting nor auto-flagellation, will change the situation.

The ego never knew real oneness with the mother, since that experience was pre-egoic. It was not a sin at all, but innocence of Eden before the opposites of good and evil, male and female, entered the mind, before the phallic phantasy, the serpent, poisoned our sexuality with shame. And all the succeeding sins were committed by a false self, a privation of Being, the same demonic force-field that collectively threatens the planet, and that can only be defeated by the power of the Truth that is Love. The God who has gone missing must now be born in every heart.

There is one easy way out of the trap that constitutes human history: a simple shift from *puer* to pure. The puerile ego must surrender its facile pornographic consciousness for the pure-know-gratitude of prayerful presence. This requires hardcore recognition that the ego itself is complete fantasy: it never existed in the first place.

The absolute evacuation of the sense of I, the realization that all that has ever been is presence, unborn, sexless, parentless, Other-less awareness—liberates from the need for liberation that is the last illusion. In the utter immolation of the porn-egoic prison, life is divinized once more, and the Self returns, eternally youthful, as the endless miracle of all that is.

Sat Yoga:
Biophysics *Avant La Lettre*

A Sat Yogi is a biophysicist—in fact, more precisely, a biophysics experiment. A Sat Yogi is someone who has had enough of the ordinary way of living life on the surface, chasing petty or futile pleasures, and who has left behind the old values based on conventional egoic notions of fulfillment that have clearly proven false. A Sat Yogi has discovered there are unsuspected potentials in the consciousness carried by the biophysical vehicle that seemingly propels him through being-time. By turning his attention inward and activating those potentials, he makes his life into an experiment in ultimate truth.

Yogis have for over 4,000 years been the world's most intrepid investigators into the realm of pure consciousness. While most people take life, the body, and the physical world for granted, the Sat Yogi, by an inward auto-attuning process of increasing refinement, bathes in the wonderment of the living energies, the subtle sublime feelings, the ecstatic vibrations, emanating from the depths of conscious presence. He attends to both the flows and the discontinuities of the realms of experience (the external, dualistic dimension), imperience (the inner world of dreams and other psychic manifestations), and sumerience (the nondual Absolute), ceaselessly astonished by the strangeness of the phenomenal dimensions, the esoteric treasures hidden in plain sight and too familiar for consideration by those with flattened consciousness still veiled by the dogmatic images of representational thought.

The Sat Yogi's ongoing experiment in living in ultimate freedom eventually encounters all the potentialities latent in the infinite field of Be(com)ing. And the Yogi learns gradually the non-obvious relationship between Being and seeing, between interconnective thinking and interconnected phenomenal appearance— apprehending the dynamics of the virtual, the unmanifest essences, within the temporal forms of the passing actualities.

Biophysics can be considered a contemporary synonym for the ancient esoteric concept of spirituality. Biophysics is a more exact term than spirituality, the meaning of which has been obscured by all the conflicting layers of religious dogma. By adopting a scientific term that is free of such baggage, the Sat Yogi auto-empowers aware action to conduct increasingly innovative research into the non-ordinary, the apparently impossible, without the constraints of a scientistic paradigm or attachment to a predetermined outcome.

All legitimate research requires radical openness to what is (including to new concepts of is-ness), and to what is possible or virtually present that cannot be objectively perceived. All assumptions must be questionable. The Sat Yogi self-authorizes the right to question, to wonder, to re-signify, to transform, to realize, to invoke, and to manifest what may be unimaginable to others— but that may be downloadable or phenomenalizable from the morphogenetic field potentials that surround and pervade us. Radical openness means freedom from veils and taboos against knowing, whether they come in the guise of religion or science, of narcissism or negativity.

Because we are alive, our first wonderment naturally concerns life itself. We find ourselves embedded in *bios*, in a body that is alive, that flows within a *phusis*, an ordered cosmos of interactive phenomenal entities resonating in a dimension of space-time consciousness. Yet how many of us have seriously asked ourselves the question, what is life? Or, what could it become?

Science has failed to bring life-and-thought energy fully into its purview as an object of study. What is the nature of this energy that enables the body to move, to think, to feel, to dream, to be aware? And what is it that causes this energy sometimes to be low and sometimes high? Why are we sometimes elated and other times depressed or anguished?

Could it be that the answer does not lie at the level of neurochemistry, which may be only an effect rather than a cause? Are there perspectives that lie beyond the usual gross materialist or even the more subtle cognitive or psychoanalytic suspicions— energy pathways that may open doorways to the deeper dimensions of our Being? Can the flow of life energy be protected, optimized, raised to levels unimagined by the collective symbolic order?

And a further question: what is a body truly capable of, what potentials does it have, if this energy of life and consciousness is focused and channeled creatively, uninhibitedly, and wholeheartedly, in ways that conventional attitudes have no clue about? Do I dare discover the greater Self beyond and within my petty personal self? Dare I advance beyond the known boundaries of possibility, to enter realms of mystery from which I might not return—or at least that might make me inconceivably different from what I thought I was—including not being an "I" at all? Confronting these questions is the essential first phase of the biophysics program of Sat Yoga.

The Sat Yogi recognizes that experimentation with *bios* means transformation of existence itself, entering into dimensions of awareness that may reveal both personal subjectivity and the objective world to be utterly non-real. Depersonalization into formless, pure awareness: This is the price to be paid for the act of creation. What is the benefit? There are many. Among them are fearless, timeless, dispassionate containment of all the contents of consciousness, as well as the gratification that flows from opening a path toward the metamorphosis of the human species as a whole, which in religious discourse would be referred to as the salvation of all souls—and toward the manifestation of a physically transformed Earth, one that will vibrate at a higher frequency than in the current phase of its movement through cyclic being/time.

Long before the advent of the modern discipline of quantum physics, Yogis were well aware of what is now being referred to by such terms as morphogenetic fields, dark energy, dark matter, black holes, the zero point field, quantum undecidability, nonlocal effects, quantum entanglement, transcosmic interconnectivity, wormholes through space, time travel, multidimensionality, even string theory. Yogis do not require any expensive laboratory apparatus, however, for their experiments. The body/mind is deployed as a quite sufficiently miraculous transducer of quantum effects.

What gets in the way of the skillful deployment of Yogic capacities—and even acts as a barrier against Yogic biophysics research itself—is the malfunctioning of the brain mechanism due to a glitch in the cognitive/conative software, a bug that is known as the ego. Yogis must first remove this glitch in the system to be able to activate the higher potentials of Being. In most human organisms, the ego occupies the dominant frequencies of consciousness and prevents the taking of reparative action.

Sat Yogis must learn to de-bug their own system, and in the process they acquire the skill to help others do so. In that sense, a Sat Yogi can be considered a bio-technician. Yogis upgrade the psychic software to enable the cerebral hardware to function at its full potential.

The upgrade leads to serenity and effortlessness, on the one hand, and unpredictability and spontaneous creativity, on the other. The mind learns to eliminate any identitarian tendencies as they arise, morphing continually into self-dissolving-awareness, quantum wave-flow presence, oscillating into and out of the zero-point field of pure potentiality. Consciousness thus enters the realm of the miraculous.

Through the application of advanced Yogic processes of concentration, the attention is fully focused within the Ground of the Real. The Absolute, Brahman, can be inadequately conceptualized as the non-localizable field of transfinite potentiality, the eternal and the virtual, giving virgin birth to the flow of becoming, appearance, phenomenality—Brahman is the unified field of All and Nothingness that flowers into universes, of which each of us is one—and many.

All of us have the power to directly discover the Absolute through the intensive practice of contemplative presence. Sat Yoga research has demonstrated that the unified field of Brahman is the realm of ultimate liberation. Liberation is freedom from the oscillation of life-and-death, but not by transcending life and death, but rather through realizing life-and-death as such. The elimination of the illusion of an ego passing through life and death, the seeing of these phases of existence as a single whole, dissolves the mirage of an entity suffering the flying-by of time.

Moreover, the indescribable revelation of truth includes the realization that at the heart of life in the phenomenal plane lies death (at the heart of which again is life, the two forces endlessly copulating in yin/yang kaleidoscopicality), and that only through death, individual, societal, and planetary, is life resurrected in its pristine perfection, as part of the eternal cycles of cosmic process that yield ever greater wisdom and bliss, until the Self and Death and Life are recognized as one. We are all at play in the field of Brahman.

Sat Yogis, in their sensitivity to the initial conditions of reality, have deduced the following formula:

$$B = RA\ (HM)/A\ \{N\}.$$

This can be translated as: Be(com)ing equals Radiant Awareness functioning as Harmonic Mind configured by Archetypes manifesting as the formative matrix of Nature.

This ancient formula, discovered several millenia ago by India's indigenous biophysical researchers, paradoxically can only now reappear and produce its full miraculous effects, if followed with precise karmic accuracy to its ultimate logical conclusions. Only now are the conditions right and necessary for new planetary creation, the quantum wave-field of consciousness having fully collapsed into forms that have decayed and degraded to the point of psychobiological exhaustion.

This golden opportunity for renewal, however, requires fulfilling the laboratory conditions in which the remaining subtle energies of life can be focused, concentrated, refined, isolated into their essential waveforms of radiant light and pure awareness, and fused by the synchronous action of the cerebral bi-hemispheric conscious particle accelerator, to the final point of implosion into Atman's primal Chidakashic Field (the microcosmic psycho-space in resonance with the Intelligence of the universal Ground)—to be followed by a re-explosion as new, extraordinarily and divinely beautiful forms of art/life/cosmos—the Logos manifesting in flesh of stardust the awesome perfections of archetypal aesthetics. This fundamental experiment in biophysics is the primordial human function, justifying our Being for inclusion in a new cycle of existence.

Ironically, the human capacity for biophysical renewal through radical Yogic neuro-plasticity is emerging at the very moment of terminal decay, paralysis, and petrifaction in most fields of thought. Particularly in biology, mainstream thinking has become bogged down in its nineteenth century Darwinian ideology, unable to integrate the insights of quantum physics into a grander vision of evolutionary bio-manifestation. Out of a misplaced fear of the return of church-imposed dogmas upon the freedom of thought, scientists have imposed their own dogmatic blindfold, one that is having even more perverse effects upon social and scientific conditions. But all this is part of the same cosmic process of death and rebirth.

The moment has thus come for the re-emergence of the singularity re-initiating planetary conditions through the vibratory emanation of a far higher wavelength than is currently resonating, producing extraordinary new forms of both virtual and actual life. Once more, through the return of consciousness to its Primal Source, our virgin zero-point potentiality is birthing a new biophysical reality in harmony with the archetypes of divinity. God's will is being done on Earth, as it always is in the virtual realm called Heaven.

The Four No-Bull Truths

One condition for the achievement of freedom from suffering is an accurate paradigm of the situation in which consciousness is seemingly trapped. Because of the 'sensitive dependence on initial conditions' that is an inherent aspect of conscious functioning, it matters profoundly what assumptions are made at the outset of a spiritual process, the aim of which is ultimate liberation.

In pursuance of such a facilitative paradigm, it is worth examining the basic assumptions of Buddhism. (Of course, we must not accept as a basic assumption that there is such a thing as Buddhism, when in fact there are many Buddhisms.) To begin, let us recall the "four noble truths" that form the starting point of early (Theravada) Buddhist teachings. The first truth is that all life is suffering (*dukkha*). The second concerns the arising of suffering, which is ascribed to thirst or craving (*tanha*). The third declares that cessation of suffering is possible, through the achievement of *nirvana*. And the fourth sets out the eightfold path that will lead one to *nirvana*.

A contradiction is uncovered, however, when one asks the question: who suffers? Buddha reveals that only a self can suffer, but that in fact there is no such thing as a self. Any kind of self is purely illusory. But if that is so, then surely its suffering is likewise illusory. How, then, can the first noble truth be true? Buddha's initial assumption seems to posit a ratification of egoic illusion. (In the later Mahayana forms of Buddhism, this issue is clarified: What Buddha meant was that for those in illusion, life is suffering. But

173

still, the question remains: Why look at reality from the perspective of illusion, when by definition that cannot offer ultimate truth? This question has led to the so-called Two Truths doctrine.)

It is a simple matter of logic: suffering is a property only of illusory selves. Buddha teaches that there is no self. Therefore, in truth, there is no suffering. The first noble truth seems to support the illusion of egoic suffering. Yet, Buddha teaches that there is a higher truth that suffering is only a secondary phenomenon that derives from ignorance of the essential nature of reality: pure rapture. Rapture is primary, because it is the essence of both Being and Nothingness. Buddha understood this, and so the first noble truth must be accepted as a teaching that is in accord with the limited intelligence of the ego, rather than an expression of the truth of the Absolute.

The remaining three truths must be seen in the same light. The second proposition regarding the arising of *dukkha* implies that thirst (meaning craving, desire, or driven-ness) is the root of the problem. And it may have been so in Buddha's time. But today, ironically, many people suffer from precisely a lack of desire, a failure of the capacity to form an intention, of the ability to motivate themselves to action. There is apathy and inertia rather than thirst for life. Even in many cases where craving seems to be the problem, it turns out upon deeper analysis to be a defense against a more profound fear of real desire. Therefore, thirst cannot be the primary cause of suffering. The root of the problem goes deeper.

The third truth, *nirvana*, must also be understood as a response to the prevailing egoic tendencies of the time. But for many today, relief from suffering is not to be had simply by blowing out the flame of desire. Suffering for many is a function of hopelessness and despair in the face of a dying world. Others suffer from a sense of utter insignificance or unworthiness, or from unconscious conflicts that they can put no words to. There is also the suffering of feeling unable to desire. Some suffer because they cannot create a loving intimate relationship with another. Advising those bearing such torments in their souls to become desire-less may lead them to pave over the dead-zone of their heart instead of healing the very root of the pain. Rather than blowing out the flame of desire, it may be better to nurture it and transform its energies into their full flowering as divine love and creative power.

So, desire is not the problem—in fact, desire (in its immaculate mode of desire by and for Nothing) is part of our essential nature. The problem is caused by identification. It is identification that leads both to futile, defiling desires and to the collapse of desire. The question is how to cut off identification.

The fourth noble truth tries to provide a solution, by offering a path of purification of desire. The eightfold path may turn a vicious ego into a more virtuous ego, assuming the vicious ego is virtuous enough to follow it. (The eightfold path is comprised of right understanding, right thought, right speech, right action, right livelihood, right effort, right mindfulness, and right concentration.) But the ego is clever, and it can use any path for its own purposes. No cognitive/behavioural program will bring about the extinction of egoic identification, since the ego's operating system lies mostly beneath the conscious level, and will not be 'blown out' even by deep meditations that reach *nirvana*. In fact, the ego can become very proud of being on a spiritual path. This can create the famous 'golden handcuffs' situation of the ego that is so proud of its ethical and spiritual superiority that it would not dream of giving up its identification with its holiness. This is what one Tibetan Buddhist teacher has called spiritual materialism, the reification of purity into the obstacle of 'higher *dukkha*.'

The need to rise beyond the plane of the ethical, epitomized by the first six steps of the Buddhist eightfold path, has been noted in modern Western philosophy, for example, in Kierkegaard's "religious suspension of the ethical," and in ancient philosophy at least as far back as Aristotle's *Nichomachean Ethics,* wherein it is recognized that the merely ethical, no matter how impeccably virtuous, does not bring true happiness. Transcendence of the ego, through contemplation of, and union with, the Absolute, can alone be the true aim of the human spirit. Of course, the Buddhist eightfold path aims at precisely that, but the thought-construct of 'path' inherently connotes a being making efforts to attain something *a posteriori*, which undercuts the *a priori* nature of liberation. This conundrum was eliminated from Buddhist discourse by the great Zen master Dogen, who cut through the knot with the paradox of *shusho-itto*, the realization that meditation practice itself is enlightenment. This is because it is a deliberate act of dis-identification.

The effort to meditate is difficult for most people, since the ego mind will not subside without a struggle. The problem of method is further compounded by the fact that most identifications function below the threshold of consciousness, and are thus not amenable to removal through the process of meditation alone. This is recognized by every spiritual tradition, of course. The solution must consist of a multi-modal approach that maximizes moments of dis-identification, augmented by the cultivation of an attitude of ego-less compassion; aided by analysis of unconscious identifications as revealed in dreams and symptoms; and ultimately the egoless Self must be brought to life by commitment to altruistic actions of service, most effectively in harmony with a vibrant spiritual community. Through the synergies of communal action, the flame of divine love that is in each member is joined to all the others, building a great bonfire. To achieve such a community, however, each member must dis-identify from the separative ego.

In light of these issues, including the changed circumstances and different types of ego-structures from those that appeared during Shakyamuni Buddha's time, a revised version of the four noble truths is offered—one we think the Buddha would agree with—instantiating a new set of initial conditions for the rapid emergence of whole buddha-communities liberated from ego. Our candidates for the set of four "no bull" truths are as follows:

1. All is rapture.
2. Rapture is veiled by the act of (mis)identification.
3. Rapture is renewed through the act of radical dis-identification.
4. No path is possible or necessary—but it is inevitable.

Let us examine these four no-bull truths more closely.

All is rapture.

Rather than beginning our spiritual process with the egoic illusion of suffering, let us begin with the enlightened truth of rapture. All of life, all that comprises the Real—including both Being and Nothingness—is of the essence of bliss itself. Note that not just life, but death as well, is included in the rapture. Even egoic suffering is included. Beneath the surface of our *dukkha*, and permeating it fully, the rapture is present unabated. We need only pierce the non-existent veil of our egoic identities, and the energies of divine intelligence, love, and joy instantly diffuse through consciousness.

We are constantly floating in a sea of rapture, but we hold onto our icon of suffering—the ego—to prevent ourselves from falling into the bottomless depths of Emptiness. This is the strange, estranged situation of human unreality. We have exchanged our essential nature of transpersonal presence for a delusion of egoic security that is actually destroying us, and destroying our natural environment, from which we have likewise become alienated. We are in a hell realm, neither phenomenal nor noumenal, lacking substance, lacking peace. Yet at every moment, the rapture is palpably present if we but have eyes to see and a heart to feel.

Rapture is veiled by the act of (mis)identification.

It is the simple mistake of identifying our presence with a material vehicle, with a mirror image, with the attitudes of others (including identification with what the psychoanalyst Jean Laplanche calls the enigmatic signifiers of the Other's desire), with collective prejudices and paradigms, with a private myth, with language itself, which produces the loss of rapture. Identification yields suffering. Identification with the gross body—the *anna-maya-kosha*, or the food body—creates disturbances throughout all our seven bodies. The entire *pranic* energy field is affected—the mental body, the wisdom body, and all the other bodies up and down the line.

The mental body is further destabilized as a result of being modified by the introjections of the desires, demands, and envious attacks of others, combined with suppressed phantasies of omnipotence and seductive power, and defense mechanisms that may include imaginary or actual disfiguration. The outcome of the disturbance in the flow of *pranic* energy is one or another sort of destabilization, producing states of too little and too much. At extreme levels, bipolar disorder can be induced. Brain circuits can be blown out. Systemic problems can occur at the organismic level. A condition of lostness destroys our clarity. Once awareness has been interpellated into a trance of co-dependent identification, there seems to be no longer a way back to the lost rapture.

The rapture is occluded by the pseudo-entityhood that separates one from the Nothingness that contains All. Once a complicated ego structure has been formed out of the above-listed elements, introjected from the projections of other illusory entities, our minds become riddled with conflicts and chaos. The flow of love is cut off by fear, anger, and confusion. The ego can stabilize itself by introjecting a strong superego, but at the further cost of guilt, shame, and a sense of inferiority. This in turn produces envy and hatred. The unbearable brew is then hidden and compensated for by the further construction of a superiority complex, abetted by splitting-off and projection of negative feelings and judgments. Sexual urgency and aggression burgeon as channels for the energetic overflow. At some point, the ego loses its ability to hold itself together. Until one takes the fateful step of dis-identifying and detaching from the ego, life remains a horror.

Rapture is renewed through the act of radical dis-identification.

The solution to the whole problem—in fact, to all the problems we face at every level of our reality, from the most intimate to the most global—is simple: radical dis-identification from all forms of egoic illusion. But in what does this consist? Utter dis-identification is unthinkable to ordinary ego-consciousness. It implies far more than mere detachment from things. It implies, at a first pass, the recognition of the failure of both sense perception and cognition as such to achieve a rapprochement with the Real.

Dis-identification requires a sloughing off of the categories of rational thought, eschewing the habit of breaking reality into a myriad of objects in spacetime orbiting a subject of experience dispersed into a succession of moments, held together only by a regulative ideal of unity based on assumed continuity of memory. With an appreciation of how the process of reification functions to de-vivify, and how the illusion of linear temporality works to pseudo-substantialize, and how profane crypto-factualization operates to erase the miraculous dimension of the Real, subjectivity can gradually shed its embeddedness in a nest of fictional obligations and expectations—at least long enough to breathe deeply of the nothingness upon which it rests and discover itself in free fall.

The subject, in full realization of its unknown-ness to itself, discovers its perpetual dehiscence not as a wound but as an unbounded openness to the mystery that cannot be spoken or contained. If awareness retains the courage to penetrate into the ultimate emptiness in which all perspectives dissolve, and all the tools of thought are allowed to fall away in the pure nakedness of the dreamflow, all things come together again in a vaster oneness of luminous delight, a knowing that is not thinking but presence, the primal fire that does not burn itself: the Rapture.

No path is possible or necessary—yet it is inevitable.

If one is in a state of mis-identification with a false self (represented by self-images and self-concepts), then it is impossible to have right understanding, let alone right mindfulness and right concentration, or even right thought, speech, and action. The ego will interfere with karmic accuracy and sooner or later will unwittingly enter into some kind of defiled entanglement. The eightfold path, or the more ancient *yamas* and *niyamas* of the original Yogis, are a wonderful guideline, but the path cannot be truly followed until egoic identification has been dissolved.

Paradoxically, once dis-identification occurs, no path is necessary. Right action happens spontaneously, rather than as part of a program or discipline. This, however, does not mean that the effort to commit to spiritual disciplines should not be undertaken. Rather, it is to emphasize that the surrender of egoic identification—and all the emotional baggage that comes along with it—is the core discipline.

Moreover, it is useful to recognize that it is inevitable that this will occur. It is part of the divine *lila*, the cosmic play of consciousness, to lead every being to Buddhahood, to Self-realization and Rapture. A point will arrive when one's spiritual path becomes not an option but an irresistible force of its own. That is called, in theistic discourse, being caught in the hands of the living God. Once the Dharma Raja, the Supreme Judge, has summoned you face-to-face in the court of Truth, the path becomes a simple forced-choice between salvation and damnation. The wrathful deities are no joke. It is better to dance with a benign Buddha or to fly with angels than to be flayed by angry demons. Either way, dis-identification will result. This realization will inevitably make the path crystal clear even to a hardened ego.

Addendum: The act of dis-identification will most easily transpire in the seven metamorphic fields of liberation, in which consciousness can take refuge from the ego's identificatory drive.

Dis-identification is unique, an act that cannot be performed by a person, or a soul, or a being of any sort. It consists in the ending of the illusion that such a being exists. Therefore, as said above, no path toward that goal is available to any being, and neither is such a path necessary. No one can perform this redeeming act, yet the conditions for its emergence can be cultivated through active participation in the seven metamorphic dimensions of liberative potentiality.

The first dimension is *transcendence*, the inward space of meditation, the intra/infra-subjective presence to the functioning of the identogenic mind. Inner silence, or samadhi, gradually impels the dropping away of all conscious identifications.

The second dimension is that of *transformation*, the field of truth-seeking inter-subjective relationship. In this space, consciousness can absorb the felt-sense of being fully apperceived. It responds by working through the functioning of language, affect, and insight stimulated to reflection by the 'in-counter' with a non-ordinary Other. If that Other empathically contains and transforms projections and other radiant emissions and is benevolently sensitive to the covert insistences of fragmentary figments of identified energy, all illusions can gradually be dissolved in the reciprocity of the dreamflow.

The third dimension is that of *translation*. This refers to the paradigm shift that translates reality into an astonishing realization of the Supreme Mystery. Although there can be no description of the undescribable Real, yet the Real is reachable precisely when reason achieves the realization of its impotence, thus dissolving all previously fixed meanings and perspectives into free and open horizons of presence.

The fourth dimension is *transfiguration*. This refers to spontaneous, egoless action. In the state of pure presence, the organism engages in action that is non-action, the *wu-wei* spoken of in Taoism. In this state of true Being, the body performs while awareness simply witnesses the performance, without taking either credit or blame. Having achieved true dispassion, the Self manifests as spontaneous flow of wonder and grace.

In the fifth dimension, *transvaluation*, the Real is recognized as not being composed of objects, beings, or things, nor even subjects as agents-operating-in-the-world. Instead, reality flows as the unending revelation of the One-without-a-second. There is only the Self, formless and therefore non-existent yet present everywhere, manifesting as the myriad of forms and phenomena of the cosmic dreamflow. Consciousness spontaneously values every moment in accord with its essential significance in the sublime aesthetic of the supreme Revelation. The separate personal perspective unites with the realization of Absolute Emptiness to birth the transfinite paradox of the priceless value of all beings, while continuing to recognize difference and division as an expression of the process that is the divine play in its birthing of the kingdom of God, the Pure Land of Amida Buddha.

The sixth dimension, *transmutation*, is that of the radiance of the highest frequencies of divine energy, the process of re-installing those energies into depleted forms for healing and renewal. This leads to complete transparency of the subtlest forces and entelechies at work in the dreamflow, observed from the locus of the arising of Suchness from the zero point of nirvanic Emptiness. The awareness of the interface between the limited and the unlimited requires the acceptance of the Self as Absolute Nothingness—the container and substance of all that is—while engaged in awakened compassionate action in the field of spacetime and its illusions of materiality. What the illusory ego sees as tragic is recognized as the very essence of Buddha-nature: impermanence. This recognition, acceptance, and full surrender to the process of evolution at the most profound levels of understanding bring the transmutation of the elements of Nature to fulfillment.

The seventh dimension, *transfinity*, arises after piercing the zero point, as realization dawns that the Self is transfinite presence of the Zero/One timelessly at play as time itself, everywhere and nowhere, the Absolute Source and the Transfinite Whole, utterly absent yet completely enrapturing. The letting-go of the final question, the highest intention, and the last illusion unveils the dawn of Supreme Liberation. The world is freed to reveal itself once more as the perfect mirror of the Perfect Self.

In sum: There is no path to the Rapture that you are, because you are already That, here and now, forever. All this shall be revealed in time. Time is eternity in motion, the cosmic dance that delivers us to and from evil, and returns us at last to our lost glory of celestial radiance. Time shall restore all things to pristine beauty. And yet eternity is inherently momentary, and it too shall appear to be lost again, through decay and death and egoic misperception. Through all the permutations of pain and pleasure, loss and gain, we can keep eternity present through undying faith and love. Love is liberation from ego. It is the ultimate gift. Love is the Rapture.

Critique of Pure Rapture

The opposite of rapture is reification. If not for that strange tendency of consciousness to objectify itself and the whole flow of experience, we would all be blissful, always. But human consciousness, with rare exceptions, at this moment in history is in a state of self-alienated, multi-track, chaotic, representational delusion.

The normal psychic structure refuses to accept the suchness of what is, the fullness and the emptiness of pure awareness. Instead, there is an urge to pretend to a pseudo-substantiality, to think of oneself as an objective identity, which requires constant maneuvers of deception. The mind selects out what can be appropriated from the Real to gain a false sense of control over the other and the world.

The ego mind unreflectively asserts its power to convert the flow of experience into idiosyncratic signifiers, labels, fantasies, and delusional hypostases. The mind is determinedly determinate, making particles out of the waveform of the Real, misidentifying consciousness itself with a limited thing, a body with a personality.

Consciousness liberated from reification is rapturous. Once reified, suffering begins. The Sat Yogi turns the egoic mind against itself with analytic clarity, so that consciousness is again recognized as original *nirvanic* wholeness, and thus is released from the travail of karma.

This travail, the loss of our original bliss and the beginning of the tragicomic reign of the oafish ego, took place in time. In fact, time is its symptom. Time is an artificial construct of the ego. It is not some inherent attribute of Nature. When the mind overcomes its addiction to reification, a different kind of time—and timelessness—is revealed.

There was, in fact, such a time before our current kind of time began, that does not show up on the conventional timeline of history, but is part of our mythic heritage. This was an age when consciousness had not yet reified itself into the otherness of body-egos, when all were one in a timeless dance of love and harmony. That was the legendary golden age, Sat Yuga, an eon that corresponds to the time known by science as Pangaea, when all the continents were unified into a single landmass, a time before the famous Flood, before the Fall of the gods. The remnants of that time include some extraordinary ruins, some unexplainable archeological phenomena, synchronous legends and cross-cultural mythemes, but nothing that can be considered proof positive. Yet there are also subjective remains of that time, buried within the unconscious minds of old souls who sometimes still have flashbacks from that era, or longings for its return. Sat Yuga exists even now *in potentia*, as a strange attractor, configuring our collective destiny by curving the space of our consciousness toward its re-enactment, until that most beautiful cosmic season returns once more.

Sat Yuga is a timeless moment when all the powers of Light are in complete alignment, creating a heavenly world, eternal yet transient, an epoch of peace and grace. Humanity will again reach its highest pitch of scientific and technological capability, but together with the most sublime nobility of spirit, aesthetic creativity and perfection, and unity of love and joyous harmony among all beings. How will it come about? A Sat Yuga occurs whenever the planetary cyclic unfoldment of consciousness reaches an ultimate impasse, when the false self filled with greed and aggressivity has colonized the collective heart of Man, when a deadlock between egoic powers has been reached that prevents the continuation of civilization, and the drive toward collective suicide culminates in an apocalypse.

We are approaching the final confrontation that will result in the full unveiling of the Supreme Real. It is occurring now, every day the screw turns a little further. The human ego has reached exhaustion, and can find no escape from its own lethal logic that is leading to the destruction of the natural world. In the collective ego's inability to save itself, paradoxically, lies the seed of salvation. This is the moment when the cry from the Heart of Nature Herself is bringing the Supreme Self to descend into the phenomenal realm to rein in the demonic human consciousness, and to reign in glory as the crown of Her own creation.

We are, without knowing it, orbiting around the unseen Central Sun that is the transcendental source of the visible universe. It functions as what the late Terence McKenna used to call 'the transcendental object at the end of time.' The teleological power of the Cosmic Self operates to draw into Itself magnetically the very flow of spacetime. As we enter the force field of that ultimate power, ego consciousness will be overwhelmed. Supernal energies will rush into every brain, will reverberate through every atom of the planet—and permeate the noetic field of Gaia as a whole. The force of this penetration by noumenal radiance will unleash a geological, biological, and psychological vortex that remakes the face of the planet. It will leave in its wake a total renaissance of life forms bursting into manifest reality.

The sages of the ancient world all held that a Sat Yuga shall come round again when we humans, or at least a sufficient number of us, once more prove worthy to live in rapture, rather than stewing in paranoid critical judgment of ourselves and one another. Cynical egoic minds cannot accept such a thought, of course, and so we shut it out of our minds and continue with the false assumption that life was always full of suffering and evil and there is no point in trying to change it. That is the self-fulfilling, depressive mentality of the current age. It too shall prove to be impermanent.

So let us understand how this delusional sufferogenic ego came about. A gradual increase in the tendency toward reification occurred as a result of the slow lowering of the vibrational frequency of consciousness, a process known in physics as entropy. In that process, language lost its link to the Absolute. Signifiers lost touch with their signifieds. The alphabet replaced the Alpha and Omega of the Real. The written word was invented, separating us further from the sensual manifold, and the self-complexifying ego entered ever deeper into its narcissistic bubble littered with the literature of its private phantasies. As love retreated, the sense of insecurity increased. Defense mechanisms, aggressivity, and ignorance bloomed like algae on an infirm ocean. The transcendent dimension was finally occluded utterly by the red tide of false consciousness. Humans became exiles in a world of artificial images and words, signifying nothing.

The fall of humanity and our future rise constitute a natural process. Energy radiates from the Center, then gradually loses power and then returns to Center once again. Consciousness on this planet is now in decay, exhausted, and thus in full return. In Yogic philosophy, this return journey of consciousness is called *pralaya*. In kabbalistic terms, it is known as *t'shuvah*. Every esoteric tradition understands this process. Luminous awareness will recharge from the Source and begin the process of planetary blossoming anew. The kind of humans that will be produced then, in the next age, our paradise regained, will be very different from the sort produced now.

Human psycho-spiritual development today can be understood to occur in a series of devolving phases. The proto-ego is traumatized by a variety of factors beginning in the prenatal period. The mother's psychological instability, her anxieties and ambivalence, as well as the instability and conflictive nature of the couple relationship, create an insecure foundation for the embryonic being's entrance into life. Psychological agitation results in physical and chemical effects in the maternal womb. This is exacerbated by the unhealthy chemical matrix produced by contemporary planetary conditions due to pollution and other environmental contaminations that have become part of the organismic burden.

Added to that are generally poor birthing conditions—metallic hospital environments, inappropriate medical procedures including unnecessary caesarian sections that do not factor in the newborn's need to establish its own readiness for birth, and inadequate emotional and financial support systems for the mother, plus lack of sufficient psychological preparation of the parents for their new role as caregivers. This all adds up to difficult and angst-producing conditions in the neonate's psyche. This in turn results in a repression of the primal free awareness and the creation of a false personality to cope with the disappointment of coming into an unsafe and stressful world.

The false self is the first 'thing', an object in the hands of all-powerful 'others'. Because our language has been crafted to function as a permanent form of brainwashing into reification, this process can only be described in terms that collude in maintaining the reifying attitude. Consciousness identifies 'itself' as a thing, because of the awareness that 'it' is perceived by 'others' as a thing. 'It' then projects thing-hood on the world at large. And later experiences tend to confirm that view, which is perpetuated by the entire educational system 'it' is forced to endure.

Once the 'I' is colonized by the false idea of being an 'it', one can only sustain, at best, what the philosopher Martin Buber called I-it relationships. Even worse, they are mostly it-it relationships. This cold comfort leads to anger, cynicism, nihilism, apathy, and despair.

The spiritual journey consists in the effort to eliminate the tendency toward such reification. In the early phases of that journey, we attempt to be more authentic subjects, not simply subjectified objects. And we try to see others as subjects as well: to create what Buber referred to as I-Thou relationships. But it is very difficult to dis-identify from the body and the ego, not to mention from the world of apparent things. Moreover, as the philosopher Emmanuel Levinas has observed, the ethical imperative of absolute recognition of the Other and sacrifice of egoic agendas in favor of the needs of the Other, can no longer be met by an ego that has been born in frustration and lack of love. It has nothing to give the Other, except its own desire for death. It desires death because it cannot remove the spell of its reification by the Other.

Even the great philosopher Immanuel Kant, though he saw clearly in his monumental *Critique of Pure Reason* that what we perceive with our senses is only phenomenal appearance, assumed that there must be some real things underneath the phenomena. He sought the *ding-an-sich*, the thing-in-itself, and wondered what we are behind the phenomenal mask of psychophysical pseudo-identity. But he could not allow himself to imagine that there is no thing-in-itself, and thus he did not reach the rapture of absolute nothingness.

What we call things are only concepts grafted upon sensations and affects. There is no subject-thing observing all the object-things. But once the illusory ego has been produced as a complex self-replicating and self-aggrandizing idea in consciousness, it takes on a 'life' of its own—the original artificial intelligence masquerading as natural—and the ongoing brainwash of language maintains the hypnotic trance of reification.

The truth is this: There is no ego, qua unitary entity, but only a cluster of bio-computer programs. These are imaginary self-states made out of a binary code of memory traces of affect-bearing words and images. This produces a psychic matrix punctuated by nodes bearing variable energy differentials. These differentials result from variations in the strength of libidinal cathexes and affects connected with different signifiers that function as a graph of reality. The psychic energy differentials in turn produce rigidified channels that dam the circulation process. As a result of these halted flows, there arises a sense of lack. This in turn produces a will to suck the energies of others, and thus to dominate and control all the positively cathected nodes of energy available, eventually projected onto the whole world as people and energy resources, to assure enjoyment (sexual, aggressive, and other modalities), and above all to maintain the pretense of real existence while absolving oneself of its responsibilities. Reality becomes reduced to the status of a video game.

But as the great seers of every culture throughout history have taught, all this is simply Maya, the cosmic illusion. The creator of this illusion is not a thing. In our primitive level of consciousness limited by language, we cannot conceive of God in any way that comes close to the truth. If we wish to approach the supreme reality, we must first dispose of the layers of delusion that separate consciousness from its source in the Absolute.

This is the therapeutic function of the ancient process of Sat Yoga: reunion with essential Being. First, we must transcend body-consciousness. That is the easy part. We recognize that consciousness employs the organism as a vehicle, but the next step is to realize that consciousness-in-itself is not even a product of that organism—in the same way that a symphony heard on the radio is not a product of the radio.

The third step is slightly harder: to dis-identify even from the concept of being a soul or separate entity of any sort. Our real being is boundless, and once we attain the state of prolonged inner silence in profound meditation, awareness achieves the realization of being eternal, unconditioned, and undifferentiating presence. Once presence is unhooked from identification with both mind and body, the transfinite dimension opens.

Then comes the subtlest realization of all: Noumenal presence equals phenomenal absence. We are presence, but presence is not a thing, nor an attribute of a thing. This recognition opens the abyss of Emptiness. Awareness is nothing in itself, but functions as the irresistible attractor/reciprocal of Light. In the total fusion of Light and Awareness, the consummation of unlimited love, the creative impulse of Cosmic Intelligence sends shock waves through the universe, a vibrating orgasm of the Absolute.

Presence liberates energy from form and returns it to the primal vibration of Om—the quantum wave before its collapse into objective matter. The liberated quantum wave then will congeal once more in a wondrous new worlding of our world-dream. Light waves will whirl a world into form from formlessness, the climax of Shiva and Shakti's sublime creative dance of endless love. Ego consciousness is being danced into divine Presence and we are reborn in rapture. Once rapture is regained, there will be nothing more to critique. Indescribable beauty, love, and goodness are now to be restored on Earth.

We are at the beginning of the renaissance of rapture.

The Quantum Apostle

Quantum physics has assumed a role in current intellectual history comparable to that of the apostle Paul in the history of early Christianity. Recall that Paul never knew Jesus personally. In fact, Christ may have been for him an archetype rather than a historical individual. His declaration of a world-shaking event that shifted the meaning of reality for all beings, that is, the faith he asserted in the truth of the resurrected Christ, produced an ontological and identitarian rupture not only with pre-Christian Judaism but with the teachings of any Jewish sage upon whom the Jesus myth may have been based. He likewise broke with the Jewish-Christianism being taught by Peter and the other Judea-based disciples of the gnostic Yeshuan teachings.

Paul entered upon and transformed the historical scene on his own, unexpectedly, in an exemplary case of quantum indeterminacy and nonlocal action. After an unsought singular moment of conversion, a Jewish man named Saul disappeared and a universal teacher named Paul manifested in his body and created an original interpretation of the meaning of the life and death of Jesus—one that eliminated all content of any actual life and teachings of a Yeshua—except the fact of the resurrection itself as the newly revealed point of exception to all law, including the laws of biology and physics. The resurrection, according to Paul, proved the liberation of man from subjection to all forms of determinate law, even that ultimate law of death that seems to hold all beings in its thrall.

Is not this declaration of freedom likewise the implication of quantum indeterminacy? The difference is that Paul's declaration was of an event that the vast majority of scientifically educated people today consider a fable. On the other hand, the new apostolic succession of quantum physics is considered by the same vast majority to be an accurate description of the fundamental reality of the universe.

At the most basic level of being, that of the subatomic particle, existence is free, beyond the control or capture by law or logos. As noted by the philosopher Alain Badiou, Paul's declaration was a coded manifesto of revolution, one that inspired the oppressed peoples of the Roman Empire to leap from the affirmation of resurrection to nonviolent insurrection, and thus to endure martyrdom as their own testament to the uncrushable power and freedom of the human spirit. Later, of course, this movement was co-opted and appropriated by the dominant political system, and its revolutionary power was channeled into conservative and regressive forms. But the residual impact of the assertion of the dimension of human freedom continues as an element of tension and paradox within the institutions of Christianity.

Paul's discourse of spiritual liberation broke with both the Jewish Law—which Peter and the other Jewish-Christian disciples continued to uphold, demanding of male converts to the new cult that they undergo the Jewish rite of circumcision in order to be accepted as Christians—as well as with the esoteric philosophic discourse of the Greek schools of wisdom that proclaimed an eternal harmony among all orders of Being. (The Greek wisdom had lost its transformational potency by that time and no longer succeeded in breaking through the archetypal order into full encounter with the Unnameable Absolute.)

For Paul, the resurrection of Christ was the equivalent of a cosmic earthquake that ruptured forever the harmony of the spheres of domination that had been set up by the human ego, and opened a path once more to the naked Absolute. "In Christ, there is neither Jew nor Greek, neither male nor female," Paul exclaimed. The validity of nationalism, of patriotism, of religious tradition, of sexism and racism, of legalism, of determinacy itself, all were totally refuted by the singular act of Christ's resurrection. What Paul declared nearly 2,000 years ago has now been seconded by quantum physics.

Today, the discourse of physics has broken both with the exhausted and ossified rhetoric of conventional science—which has not yet been able to catch up with or integrate the remarkable findings of quantum indeterminacy into its evolutionary paradigm—as well as with the dogmatic and too often hypocritical discourse of conventional religion. All previous systems of belief regarding the nature of reality have thus been destabilized by the irrefutable findings of fundamental physics. These findings declare an end to the empire of egoic reason, of law, of certainty, and uphold the unknowable, uncontainable freedom of Being itself at the most basic level of the Real.

One revolutionary discourse that has *not* been overthrown by quantum physics is that of Sat Yoga, the core paradigm of ancient Indian thought (later ramified into Shaivite, Advaita, and Buddhist forms), the thread of which has covertly been interwoven into the fabric of every historic advance of free thought that underlies all the exoteric systems of religion qua social control that have dominated the world for the past two thousand years.

The Good News that is being transmitted by Sat Yogis together with the new quantum apostolate is that the resurrected Christ is actually the noumenal Self present in all beings. This quantum gospel of Sat Yoga declares that the Self is the One Absolute, the Unified Field that holographically creates, connects, and conforms all energies, entities, and information into one coherent Whole.

What is most salient today is that the Self in question has now been resurrected, by the same scientific urge to know Truth that crucified it in the first place. Long in abeyance in the collective consciousness, the power of the Supreme Source is now entering into full avataric descent. The Source of the Field is appearing in the Field in manifest form. Quantum physics, information theory, psychoanalysis, archetypal, transpersonal, and other forms of depth psychology, deconstruction, semiotics, phenomenology, psychedelics, Gaia theory, Zen and Yogic meditative practices, to name a few, are all converging upon the same ultimate reality.

But unlike conventional religions of the past, the announcement of a new dispensation by quantum physics does not imply the coming of a particular messianic being in the form of a human savior. Rather, what is implied is that the truth of our universal Being is coming into a state of collective realization. A non-ordinary, strange attractor is operating immanently yet transcendentally upon the phenomenal forces of the universe.

In other words, people today are becoming aware of informational waves of a higher order of coherence than that provided by human language. They are receiving this information in forms that range from what they call intuitions, premonitions and visions, to teaching dreams, channeling, out-of-body and near-death experiences, and the feeling of a vaster, divine presence encompassing and permeating consciousness. These kinds of non-ordinary events have always been available to those who could tune into them. Such people have been referred to variously as mystics, psychics, or yogis. But this kind of information flow is now being received, often involuntarily, by a growing number of individuals without a background in the psychic disciplines. During such events, these individuals are operating as transducers of the Unitive Field's attribute of super-coherence. This attribute is currently being distributed throughout the planetary noetic field. In the near future, according to yogic science, when a crucial threshold energy potential is attained on the planet, through nonlocal quantum-level feedback mechanisms that are rapidly reaching a peak of intensity, the 'mother wave' will generate transformative effects upon the material conditions of planetary reality as a whole.

The question for those who take up the call of the apostolic quantum is how to operationalize the new gospel of scientific salvation. This requires the complex capacity to make a simple differentiation between system and field. Each of us has installed within the neurological apparatus an ego system—a complex network of signifiers and semiotic/analytic functions matriculating homeostatically in consciousness, at and below the level of normal waking awareness—that is being affected by these higher energies. This interaction produces chemical and psychic spikes, according to the charges released by the unknown attractors embedded in both the unconscious and superconscious strata of the planetary noetic field. At critical energy thresholds, these standing waves have the capacity to activate the cognitive and motor responses of all organisms in the field, even in opposition to their conscious volition, and at lower frequencies to evoke responses that produce acute or enduring psychic and somatic effects.

But beyond the ego-systemic illusion of separate existence, the real Self consists and persists as the unifying field of pure awareness containing and elaborating all these informational waves. The energy differential between the accelerating flux and its changeless containment vessel is producing an increasingly potent wave of novelty, of unpredictable changes in the process of change itself, at all levels of reality.

The simple, yet refined act of a mature conscious being to induce dis-identification from all the phenomenological and semiological artifacts of consciousness, realizing the Self as the boundless field of pure awareness, liberates consciousness from the illusion that there is anyone needing to be liberated. This paradoxical disappearance and immanent transcendence of the ordinary logic of the collective consciousness impacts the field of human events in strange ways. At the individual level, the personal egoic nightmare comes to an end, and free life begins. At the collective level, the Logos of the current world-age is gradually giving way to the birth of a new eon. The Unified Field is effectuating its realization in and as a new cycle of time, including within it as its collective avatar a transformed planetary community, a super-organism that will function at an inconceivably godlike level of consciousness, spreading across the planet a realization of oneness, and transmitting an energetic field creating health, harmony, restored perfection of Nature, and endless delight.

The age-old concept of Sat Yuga, the kingdom of heaven on Earth, is no fantasy, but an inevitable corollary of quantum physics. The individual field of awareness, known to Yogis as Atman, is at all times holographically coherent with the universal Source Field, Brahman. Awareness is ultimately one single field of wholeness containing the entire implicate order that is the source of all quantum effects, the ground of all the waves and particles and information that make up the universe. And so, when a sufficient amount of previously bound energy returns boundless and formless to the Source Field, the Source is triggered to emanate a new cosmic dream.

The Source Field is not an entity, not even when in manifestation. Brahman is pure intelligent loving transfinite potency. Its appearance can only be localized in the form of differentiation without alienation, creativity, inspiration, delight, spontaneity, joy, faith, hope, and love. Of these, love is pre-eminent, the *sine qua non* of the new age. Love is the only law recognized by both Paul and our current quantum apostle.

Love is both the path to salvation and the power of freedom. Resurrection and rapture are emerging as our future. Prepare for the second coming of the Self.

God(s) R Us

Awakened spiritual teachers from many distinct cultures have realized the same astonishing fact: This infinitely diverse world of beings and phenomena is the expression of a single benevolent creative intelligence.

Each of us, and all of us together, are "That" ("That" referring to the Supreme Being, One Without a Second, the most obvious and present reality to the awakened, yet utterly mysterious—even preposterous—to the un-awakened human mind).

The fact of our unity as the immanent/transcendent Absolute is the key to the salvation of our world. This is a significant point, now that our planet is on the brink of destruction by the effects of the collective delusional human ego trapped in conflicted multiplicity. This most important fact, of our transcendent unity, the realization of which was the central organizing principle of ancient cultures, has been increasingly obscured by what in the East is called *avidya*, ignorance, and in the Christian tradition is called original sin. To achieve liberation from egoic delusion and the restoration of our lovely garden planet to its original Edenic beauty, we must solve the technical problem of how to realize individually and collectively the primal fact: *God(s) R Us*.

First, however, we must be clear that to say that 'God(s) r us' is not equivalent to saying that humans are gods. Quite the contrary, it is our false sense of being at the top of the evolutionary heap, and therefore able to do whatever we want to the planetary ecosystem, with no one above us to answer to, that constitutes the problem. Likewise, the delusion that we are separate, self-contained independent yet short-lived organisms, rather than a single planetary super-organism, justifies our egocentricity and veils our underlying unity.

What is potential in the vast majority has been experienced as reality in only a relatively few great awakened beings. But what Christ proclaimed—"I and the Father are one"—is possible for all of us, and that realization, that the true I is one with the Absolute, has always been the ultimate aim of religion. In order to fully live that truth, we must achieve radical self-transformation and transcendence of ego-consciousness. In other words, we must alter the way we understand ourselves and change the way our mind functions. Self-realization is not a state of consciousness. It is the presence that lies beyond consciousness. Yet the consciousness must be purified in order for the Self to manifest. Once there are no more tendencies to hide from the Self in egoic ignorance, liberation is achieved. This final outcome has been called by various names, such as *jivanmukti* (liberation while alive), Buddha-hood, and Christ-consciousness. Simply put, it is the return to whole-mind from split-mind.

We have been seeking our lost wholeness in the wrong places, by worshipping idols, the primary one being the ego itself. The ego collectively externalizes itself into a variety of other false gods— ranging from religious icons and practices to such concepts as nationalism, capitalism, democracy, communism, money, physical beauty, food, and other objects and events in the realm of the senses. All this is indeed the result of the "original sin" of eating of the tree of the knowledge of good and evil, which led to Eve and Adam being kicked out of Paradise. That metaphor refers to the mind's getting sucked into a mode of binary processing in which everything is either 1 or 0 (good or evil, black or white, believer or infidel, etc.). Once the mind falls into this trap, it can no longer perceive reality as whole—the Real is cut into innumerable pieces. Only when we have transcended split-mind and returned to whole-mind, at a higher level of understanding—post-egoic, rather than pre-egoic consciousness, retaining the fruits of differentiation and complexity, but now sublated into wholistic simplicity—will we be able to recognize the ultimate Real (God) as the immediate Real (Self) of unity-in-apparent-diversity, and thus realize the fundamental truth that God(s) r us.

As a result of falling from whole-mind into split-mind (a fall that was actually a rise, but an incomplete phase-shift), our conscious identity has been reduced to a representation of the Self, rather than its full Being. The human self-representation began as something sublime, with the charisma of spiritual royalty, but over time it has fallen to the level of the ridiculous and demonic.

A representation is one definition of a toy. Humans have become more and more cynical regarding their toy egos, as their characters have fallen into more infantile levels of narcissism. Gradually our egos have become deformed into their current demonic toy versions of our once noble selves. It is no coincidence that we are obsessed these days with our toys, because our minds have lost the power to penetrate into the depths of our innermost essence to discover the Real, and so we treat our world as if it were likewise a toy. We are pretending to be authentic, but we have nearly all become imposters. We live in imaginary worlds. So, before it can become reality again that God(s) r us, we must transcend our embeddedness in the representational plane and make it no longer the case that toys r us.

What is Real to whole-mind is impossible to split-mind. One of the truths obscured by split-mind is that multiplicity is also unity. Split-mind projects arbitrary conceptual boundaries between objects, while whole-mind sees clearly that all so-called 'things' are interconnected, a seamless whole that is far greater than the sum of its parts. By dissecting everything into parts, split-mind has killed reality, has deadened our sensitivity to the miraculous nature of our living world. In other words, we have gained apparent mastery over the physical realm via science and technology, but in the process we have lost our souls. Not only has it not profited us; worse, humanity is now bankrupt—not just spiritually, but even economically, as well as philosophically, psychologically, socially, politically, and environmentally.

To recover from this devastating loss, we must move beyond the current ideology of (pseudo)-individualism, which is one of the deadliest idols to which we have bowed down. The shadow side of the ideal of individualism is the unspoken fact that the ego today is weaker than ever, and prone to unhealthy enmeshment with others. True individuation is very different from individualism. The true individual is one who has the courage to transcend the narcissistic ego and attain oneness with the Source of our Being. To do this, the mind must renounce all thought-constructs, all grasping, all partiality and territoriality, all worry, all seeking, and all desire. We must stop acting as mad nomad monads with gonads and start thinking, speaking, and acting as manifestations of the All-encompassing God qua Nature, that is, the whole multidimensional Universe.

To accomplish this, we must purify the ego-mind of its dearest and most hidden fantasies and desires. At the core lies the desire to be worshipped. Every ego wants to be recognized and treated as a god. Paradoxically, we can only attain God-consciousness after we have shed the desire to be seen as a god. We must completely de-objectify ourselves, and renounce playing with self-toys. This profound renunciation requires complete surrender to the Real God.

When this happens, the mind realizes itself as emptiness, nothingness—the final stage of individuation. But the empty space of consciousness is filled with noumenal, all-pervading presence, and with the whole realm of phenomena. In fact, phenomena pervaded by noumenal awareness constitute the form of our emptiness. In the same way, a dream is pervaded by the mind of the dreamer. The Self does not appear in the dream (except perhaps as a symbolic representation), but pervades the dream. In the realm of physics, matter/energy derives from spacetime itself, forming out of nothing. This *creatio ex nihilo* occurs thanks to the power of the Real transcending and manifesting as the intelligent ground of spacetime, the unseen rainbow of the gravity that curves space and congeals light into matter, evolving into beings who can recognize themselves as That.

For creation to occur at any level, and for the oneness of creator, creature, and creation to be realized, an act of grace is both required and inevitable. A ray of divine light from the transcendent self-effulgent God Who dwells beyond, within, and as the all-pervading Nothingness must be recognized by the mind as Presence. The mind that opens to Presence realizes the Self as Source, and thus surrenders all other desires. Thus, the mind regains its original pristine emptiness and wholeness. Surrender to the Divine Presence is the magical act that brings about the Immaculate Conception. Into that mind-space of holy emptiness, God will descend as into a womb through which to be born into this world.

Intelligence and will both transcend the forms of mind and nature, and yet are immanent to mind and nature. When mind has attained the state of empty free cognizance (not only cognizance of phenomena, but Self-cognizance, recognition of the noumenal presence of the Absolute) then the power of grace blossoms instantaneously. In the emptiness of surrender to God, the blissful consummation of love between God and individuated consciousness fuses all into One—world, God, Self, all three are one. Those who become fully established in whole-mind, as manifestations and transmitters of the pure energy of God-essence, naturally become as gods.

The first fruits of the sustained effort to achieve whole-mind are serenity, love, wisdom, and healing power. Other powers may also be bestowed by the grace of the Supreme Intelligence, in accord with the plan that is secretly guiding the planetary process in the birthing of a perfected meta-humanity and the dying of the old, corrupted, demonic human species.

We are in good hands, but we can only know that, and participate consciously in the sacred birth process that is underway, if we shed the obsolete ego and realize the most important fact: *God(s) r us.*

After Monogamy:
The Advent of Momogamy

Our dying civilization has entered a new phase that can be thought of as the end of monogamy—and the beginning of mom-ogamy. Monogamy was an artifact of patriarchy. Now that the patriarchy has crumbled, males generally no longer enter the state of inner being once known as manhood. They remain psychologically situated as boys. As such, they also remain emotionally tied to their mothers. And as a consequence, they cannot sustain a healthy primal emotional tie with a woman. In other words, they cannot fulfill a vow of monogamy.

This condition is referred to by Jungians as the *puer aeternus* complex. It exists in varying gradations, as a spectrum of developmental possibilities. At the healthier end of this spectrum, such boy-men marry dominating women and recreate a son-mother relationship with them. Or else, the boy-man chooses a collage of women, either through serial affairs or open poly-amory, to none of whom he can make a firm commitment, while his heart belongs to mom. At the less healthy end of the spectrum, the boy can never leave home at all, remaining in a hostile fusion with the actual mother. In some cases, this is enacted and abetted through homosexual liaisons, masturbatory fantasies, or even psychotic delusions.

Under these conditions, girls generally no longer grow into women, either, at least not into what the word 'woman' used to signify. This is because of the simple fact that one cannot be a 'woman' except in relationship to a 'man'. Unless a woman can feel the thrill of being loved and celebrated by a powerful man for the fullness and grace of her femininity, the feminine essence cannot flower in the sacred act of surrender that opens her heart, enabling the life-giving power of her love to flow.

Once manhood and true masculinity have vanished from the collective consciousness as a reality, femininity must also morph into new forms. Girl-women have several options. Some remain trapped in momogamy as daughters. In the more concrete cases, such girl-women renounce their independence and live permanently in the mother's home and orbit around the mother, who remains the only love/hate object—and the constant cause of disappointment and guilt. In other cases, the girl attempts relationships with grown boys, but they usually fail, and the prodigal daughter returns to mom. Or the boy-girl pair maintain a marriage, but the primary relationship of each is still with mom, and the marriage becomes merely a source of complaints that bond mother and child even closer. In other cases, lesbian relationships are the daughter's only path away from home.

In the cases where the girl-woman does achieve relatively successful marriage and childbearing, it is usually by virtue of accepting the projections of a boy-man who apperceives her as the omnipotent phallic mother. She can live off those projective identifications, fueled by the energy produced by such phantasmatic mirroring, but because the husband is de-legitimized as an Other, she will constantly need to augment his gaze with the projections of others who likewise put her on a pedestal as superwoman. This could require affairs or other kinds of unhealthy relationships that will produce a residue of guilt and anguish.

Furthermore, because of the defensive pretense involved, based on a phallic phantasy, there can never be sufficient proof that she is truly who she claims to be. Thus, her pedestal becomes a treadmill, as she runs non-stop after her fleeting ideal image. She is forever needy for the neediness of others. She will generally have to make her children into weaklings who depend on her throughout their lives, and who thus must not leave home, or if they do, they must not succeed in life and thus no longer need her to be their rescuer. She will choose needy and dependent friends, and not be able to get too close to people. She can never put down her guard.

As the culture falls into *de facto* matriarchy, there are rear-guard actions to support the atavistic version of manhood and monogamy, particularly from the traditional bastion of monotheistic religion. But this hollowed-out mythology has devolved into a rigid and hyper-aggressive form that can only produce a caricature of manhood, a stereotyped imitation of a sort of manhood that existed in past centuries, but not the strength of real manhood that can meet the exigencies of our unprecedented historic moment. And no woman can depend on it, because its artificial nature tends to break down into oppressive misogyny.

Nor can matriarchy provide an alternative. Unlike the mythic matriarchies of pre-historic millenia, the current informal one is not sustainable. In the ancient world, the archetype of the Great Mother Goddess was alive and well, and conferred a collective power upon the female. The social context entrained male energies into a constructive supportive role, and sexuality could be expressed joyously. Yang could wholeheartedly serve Yin. Today, by contrast, the ascendancy of the female is not accompanied by the ascendency of the feminine. Women and men denigrate each other, in a pseudo-phallic battle for the pedestal of alpha person, or one party submits, but becomes emotionally frigid or impotent. It has become a given in most relationships that there is no true love to be exchanged between man and woman. Aggressivity has replaced affection. In the refusal/inability to love, we have lost our essential humanity. Our evolution has gone into reverse.

This, of course, is the death knell of our civilization. So what is a girl or guy to do? Gender confusion cannot be resolved by homosexual evasion of relationship with the other sex. Nor can it be resolved through so-called "trans-gender" identification—or worse, by surgical shifting of sexual positioning. On the individual level, one must develop the psychological capacity to achieve what adulthood used to mean. It takes courage to love. It takes courage to be a real woman. It takes courage to be a man. It means giving up the immature focus on playing with body parts or being babied by a mother figure. It means overcoming ambivalence and making a wholehearted commitment. That requires emotional stability, perseverance, understanding, compassion, detachment, decisiveness, the capacity for solitude, the patience and strength to endure lost causes, and the wisdom to know when to move on. All these virtues come out of a deep connection to the inner source of ultimate gratification and wholeness. One must transcend the futile desire to be made whole by a human Other.

Spiritual completeness is no longer a luxury of monks and nuns, sadhus and ashram-dwellers. It is a necessity if one is to survive modern life. Wholeness, or enlightenment, which brings liberation from identification with the gender-enmeshed ego, is the highest stage of human psycho-spiritual evolution, and reaching that stage has now become an evolutionary requirement. Otherwise, the futility and lovelessness of existence on our dying planet of the apes will become unbearable. Liberation involves freedom from egoic fixations, from envy, guilt, and other forms of negativity. Enlightenment is freedom from the illusions created by the symbolizing mind. We must reach a level of consciousness that transcends the cultural constructions of male/female identification, even that of identity as a person, and thus leads beyond the impasse that entails the withholding of love.

Once one has regained the power of love, one will draw loving beings into one's life. Love may come in the form of a loving partner, or deep friendships, or a spiritual teacher, or a supportive spiritual community, or all of the above. In the ultimate state, there is transcendence of the opposites of yin and yang, and realization of oneness with the Absolute. There are no others.

In the context of a shared vision of what humanity can become, embodied in actual day-to-day living, those who have transcended the quagmire of momogamy can offer hope and a path toward the renewal of our most noble and beautiful potentialities of Being. A new era of cultural renaissance can be created, one that goes beyond the limited conceptualizations of manhood and womanhood of past ages, beyond the pale of patriarchy, toward a mutual blissful recognition of the divine splendor of the marriage of both masculine and feminine incarnations of our supreme essence. Liberated consciousness rejoices in the dance of life, dreaming one another into infinite perfection.

Incredible Shrinking Man

Yes: Man is shrinking. Mankind was once the collective incarnation of the Supreme Being, or at least made in the very image of God—the embodiment of all that is noble, just, merciful, compassionate, truthful, wise, and courageous. In the course of the millennia, we have fallen from that sublime pedestal, and our existential stature has shrunk below even that of the most deceitful animal. We humans have become, as a species, the embodiment of stupidity, egocentricity, cowardice, and blind destructiveness.

If our scientists had any honor, they would strip our species of the unwarranted title of *homo sapiens sapiens*—which implies that we are, of all beings, the wisest of the wise. Does anyone today really think we deserve such an appellation? Would any other species destroy their own world, as we are doing? No other species enjoys imprisoning, torturing, and killing other members of its own species—and justifying such acts in the name of God, Democracy, Progress, the Proletariat, or in the name of defending Liberty. Nor could any other species deliberately carry out policies leading to the destruction of the very foundation of life, upon which we depend for our own existence.

If we are going to awaken from our collective trance, in which mankind is hurtling to extinction along with that of most other species on the planet, then we must understand the nature of our self-delusion, and accede to a methodology of awakening that will rouse us quickly from our fatal slumber. We require at least a level of enlightenment that will enable us to survive and possibly recapture the greatness of our lost spiritual stature.

One way to understand the general collapse of human nobility of spirit is to see it as an analogue of another collapse that looms before us and is part of the larger picture, that of our global economic system.

In brief, once upon a time, human beings were in resonance with Nature, and we received all that we needed directly from Her. What each of us had, we freely shared with others. Our small, loosely connected, freewheeling nomadic societies were held together by an economy of love. Commerce was performed as a series of free acts of gift giving, which eventually became ritualized. The objects of utility that we created were at the same time original works of art, crafted with infinite attention to detail in states of meditative intensity. All of life was sacred; every act was an offering, a sharing of grace, and a giving back of goodness to our Mother, the Earth (mater=matter=matrix). She, the essence of Love, was recognized as the one sub-stance underlying the all-containing field of Being.

A historic shift in consciousness occurred that determined a movement away from the spirit of Love as the ruling deity. Human aspiration shifted from the focus on living in the timeless present and the joy of Being. Instead of living in relation to ineffable Quality, which is essentially incommensurable, there was an accelerating emphasis on Quantification and the new god of authoritarian Power. This shift was reflected in hierarchical forms of social organization, based on the principle of patriarchy. Accompanying this form of organization was a new form of social exchange, one based on quantifiable equivalence. This concept, of an objective general equivalent of all value, later identified with gold, gave birth to the egoic notion that has ruled humanity ever since: Profit.

With the advent of the patriarchy, women became objects of exchange. In this trade of freedom for power on the part of Man, love became the lost object of human desire. Love was made impossible by the very objectification of the female who represented it. She could no longer fully or freely offer it, as a consequence of the denial of her full human status. Men measured their profits in terms of the number and beauty of their wives, as well as their cattle and landholdings. In the debasement of women into mere objects, men also shrank into greedy, possessive tyrants, becoming progressively unworthy of love.

The degradation of woman was compensated by the creation of religious ideologies that raised the symbol of the Virgin Mother Goddess to the rank of the sublime, while thrusting actual, loving women down to the status of either chattel or whore. The archetypal Woman became the untouchable maiden, the object of chaste, courtly love; while the women who were chosen as wives, or forced by circumstance into prostitution, were denounced as 'Eves', the cause of Man's Fall. Trust shrank from what had been a universal condition of mutually loving human siblinghood, to that of a far more limited sort of collusive and homoerotic brotherhood. Woman became the dangerous Other. With this divine/diabolic bifurcation of Woman, the stature of Man as indeed a fallen being (a snake in the grass) was confirmed.

The shrinking of Man went further with the advent of warfare as the primary method of power enhancement. Trade and commerce morphed into war profiteering, eventually congealing into massive military/industrial establishments. In order to pursue the great game of empire, trade in objects could no longer be accommodated through barter. A particular object would have to be chosen to represent the essence of all Value—the lost openness to Quality, the lost presence of Love, the repressed sub-stance of our Being. The object chosen was gold. Now that the golden light of love had been extracted from our hearts, it served as a perfect metaphor for the power and radiant beauty we had eliminated from our real existence.

More and more, we learned to live in a phantasmic realm of representation, rather than in reality. The installation of paper money eliminated even gold from the world of commerce. Eventually, it was agreed that the paper money no longer even had to represent gold; it could float freely in its own psychotic world of fictional power. All value now became based on intimidation, the threat of the ultimate use of deadly force. As Mao wrote in his famous red book, power comes from the barrel of a gun. The power of love had been eviscerated from the modern world.

Because we no longer lived in a world of direct experience, but in a plane of representation, the same thing happened to language that had happened to commerce—the gold standard was eventually eliminated. No longer did words represent realities, but signifiers simply floated in a field of terminology that could be made to mean anything that those with a Voice—those with power in the social hierarchy—wanted their words to seem to mean. Discourse was disconnected from the last references to the Real—except the Real of destruction and death.

Man has entered a phase of terminal paranoid psychosis. We have been shrunken to mere substance-less, deathly, and ghostlike fragments of our former selves, less than a shadow of what we had once been. Though it may seem to some that we have made progress, thanks to various social liberation movements, such as feminism, gay rights, and racial equality, none of these movements has succeeded in bringing us closer to the lost golden heart of love, but in fact these necessary but ego-driven, non-wholistic, causes have only served to increase the levels of polarization, competition, distrust, and social strife—which are culminating in the decomposition of the last pure elements of human existence. The incredible fact is that shrunken Man is at war with himself—and he is on the brink of pulling the trigger of thermonuclear suicide. Nietzsche's idea that "God is dead" is obsolete. Now it can fairly be stated that Man is a 'dead man walking'.

Is there any hope for a revival of our true Nature, or is doomsday the inevitable end of the evolutionary trail for shrunken Man? Is there a spiritual rabbit that can yet be pulled from the hat into which Man's shrunken head has fallen? Our answer is an unequivocal Yes! It will not be easy to free ourselves from the imaginary egoic identity in which we are trapped. But it can be done. The power of Love has been denied, but its potency remains intact. We need only tap into it once more.

The teachings of the great sages, the brightest Lights of human wisdom through the ages in all spiritual traditions, the words and energies of those who stubbornly refused to shrink themselves, provide wonderful guidance for us. Those teachings can be augmented today with insights distilled from postmodern investigations into the hidden dimensions of consciousness, gathered from such disciplines as psychoanalysis and psychotherapy, semiotics, phenomenology, deconstruction, quantum physics, energy medicine, and a wide variety of body/mind practices, ranging from chi kung and aikido to pranic healing, among others. This information can, if rigorously applied in a trans-egoic paradigm, bring about psycho-spiritual redemption. We need only analyze and deconstruct the egoic defenses, dis-identify from the plane of the signifier, cast off the body-mind entirely, and concentrate in the absolute stillness of pure awareness.

If, as the mad hatter advised Alice in her Wonderland, one pill makes you smaller (the pill of the ego's will to power), then there is still the option of taking the other pill that makes you large—the transformative pill of surrender to Truth and Love. This will require on the part of each of us a massive inner effort of will to wisdom, delivering our Being from bondage to the chains of language, from addiction to the craving for the imaginary and the sensual, from the fear-and-shame based power struggles that block our capacity to love, and from the petrified bedrock of the ego's unconscious fixations. In short, we require a transmutation of identity from body/mind self-image to the eternal, formless, nameless Ground of our Being, the all-unifying Emptiness of Pure Awareness—the infinite field of Presence that is always suffused with Love and Light.

In other words, we are coming home. We are returning to our full spiritual stature that we lost in the fatal illusion of gaining power over Nature, women, and other people. We can yet become masters over the shrunken egoic mind, rather than its slaves, by simply transcending those egoic agendas and realizing the One Self that is All.

We have the power to write a new, redemptive chapter of human history: The Incredible Unshrinking and Re-Divinization of Humanity. Let us inscribe our new testament together, in the birthing of a sacred community of liberated consciousness. But we must hurry—the time left to do this is shrinking fast.

PART FIVE

The Supreme Liberation

Original Bliss

Our original and innermost nature is serene, blissful Self-awareness. This is a fact you can verify for yourself. It has been repeatedly confirmed for thousands of years by those who have made the wholehearted effort to pierce the veils of illusion and mental resistances, to re-connect surface consciousness with the core of our Being. Those who have achieved the supreme beatitude through conscious discipline have been known since the beginnings of human history as Yogis. Yoga is not a religion but a psycho-technology, sometimes referred to as meditation. Therefore, there are Hindu Yogis, Buddhist Yogis, Taoist Yogis, Christian Yogis, and so on. The science of Yoga continues to bring dedicated practitioners to the supreme state of original bliss.

The discipline of Yoga initially focused on developing methodologies of silencing the mind, and also refined the field of metaphysics, integrating the philosophy and psychology of consciousness into a rigorous and coherent practice of wakeful stillness. Yogis returned from meditative absorption in the Absolute and elaborated such concepts as *Sat*, or Being; *Brahman*, the Absolute; and *Atman*, the individual spirit, the intelligent energy behind our ego-consciousness. The Atman was recognized as the auteur of our dreams; the still, small voice of conscience; and the driver behind our urge toward ultimate liberation. The Atman, once delivered from eclipse behind the ego mind, floods the soul with the healing waves of our original bliss.

The ancient Sat Yoga of original bliss has been recovered in these latter days of human history and has been restored to full potency. Sincere practitioners of prayer and meditation in all the world's spiritual traditions have made the same discovery. Though every tradition has employed different names to refer to our ultimate reality—such as Nirvana, Emptiness, Infinite Light, Supreme Goodness, Limitless Love, Absolute Nothingness, Absolute Fullness, and, of course, the Godhead—all words are inadequate, as the richness and utterly mind-bogglingly complex simplicity of its wondrously paradoxical nature is impossible to convey in language. But all traditions and sages who have achieved the summit of meditative realization agree: our original and inherent essence is bliss.

Those who have tasted the supreme illumination testify that our original bliss is the greatest treasure that can be attained in life. It is Life itself. Once our latent bliss-filled nature has been regained, nothing more remains to be desired. It is the climax of the spiritual journey.

One day, every human being will realize this. It may be important to emphasize that the achievement of original bliss is not the end of our earthly existence. In fact, it signals the beginning of authentic living. From that moment, one can function in a state of grace and offer blessings and inspiration to all beings. Our original bliss is the natural basis for a planetary renaissance of the most sublime and harmonious community and culture imaginable.

In the past, this goal has only interested a few rare individuals, while the mass of humans have limited themselves to worldly preoccupations. Today, given the situation of the world on the brink of the abyss, the achievement of awakening to union with the Supreme Reality is no longer a luxury for monks and hermits, but is essential for all of us who want to stay sane during the coming global crack-up, to be able to guide the world to the new dawn of peace and harmony. This encompasses both biological and Gaia-logical renewal.

Over the centuries, the holy science of Sat Yoga has made many important discoveries regarding the structural resistance of the ego to enjoying original bliss. The antagonism to joy functions relentlessly in the false self as a result of its primal alienation from Atman. This splitting of consciousness gave birth to the ego in the first place. Indeed, one of the instantiating prohibitions that constitutes the mental membrane, by which the egoic consciousness is partitioned off from the infinite oceanic expanse of blissful awareness in which it heedlessly floats, is the prohibition against bliss itself. The return to blissful awareness is misperceived by the ego as a lethal threat. Indeed, it is the final undoing of the artificial sense of separation as a pseudo-individual—and the emergence of the Self of the Universe.

Yogis have always asserted that a time will come when the non-localizable Supreme Self downloads through all human brains simultaneously, at the cusp between the end of one cycle of history and the beginning of another. At that auspicious moment, which Sat Yogis claim is coming soon, we shall experience oneness as a species, in fact, oneness with all Nature, and the return of what has been called poetically the Kingdom of Heaven. Our potential for wholocentric consciousness is not a religious fantasy, but a scientific fact.

In the meantime, having lost our attunement to the vibrational frequency of the One Self, we have fallen into the angst-riddled illusion of being skin-encapsulated egos. As a result of this misbegotten mandate for misery, a barrier has been erected that is fortified by an electric fence installed in the egoic membrane. This mad defensive mechanism creates alarm and anxiety whenever one approaches the boundary-less state of utter openness. The transfinite truth of blissful Being (mistakenly feared by the ego as a desolate void) is encountered whenever consciousness begins to leave its unhappiness behind. Most often, awareness quickly falls back into the egoic rut.

Ego-consciousness cleaves to the cause of its dissatisfaction, remaining resolutely trapped in alienation and frustration. Because the conscious mind of the ego does not understand what is happening, it invents delusory rationales for its refusal of liberation and looks for crumbs of enjoyment in the realms of sensual pleasure and mental acrobatics, pleasures that inevitably come served with side orders of suffering. This is the tragedy and comedy of the human condition.

In sum, our true nature is blissful awareness, but our lives are too often lived in blind torment. We are like birds that have flown into a house and instead of flying out again through the open door, keep knocking our heads against the glass windows. We feel hopeless, separated forever from the joy we seek, though with just a small change of attitude, we can be free in an instant.

It is the narcissistic resistance of the ego to the dissolution of its imaginary selfhood that is ultimately responsible for all the conflicts in human history. It is this error that Christian dogma has labeled original sin. The unfortunate aspect of defining the human condition in that manner is that we have lost our collective understanding that the egoic illusion is not our original state, but a deterioration of an earlier state of original sinlessness that we can easily recover.

Throughout the Fall called history, the human spirit has indeed been in decline. Despite the modern secular ideology of progress, it is obvious that, from a psycho-spiritual perspective, societies have become more materialistic, egocentric, and aggressive. The ego has become thicker, crueler, more self-deceiving, more corrupt, and more fragmented. Today, there are no more barriers in the collective consciousness against the use of terror, torture, genocidal extermination, and even the use of the ultimate weapons of global destruction to hold on to the delusions of power and privilege.

This is all part of the cyclic play of time, in which human consciousness falls from good to evil, from enlightenment to ignorance and thence, through extreme suffering and repentance, to spiritual search and finally renewed enlightenment. We are nearing the final moments of the bleakest period of human corruption, hatred, brutality, and collective disinformation and poisoning of the world's natural environment. Humans have fallen to the lowest level of the utterly demonic. There is no further to fall, and so we must begin our rise again. As a species, we have lost all that is noble and good, by which we once defined ourselves as the crown of creation. Destruction is upon us. All that is left is to see the blessing hidden in this cosmic drama.

For most people, mired in cynicism, it is too much of a stretch to visualize the possibility of human redemption. It is easy to perceive the dark side of our situation, of course. Few will deny the obscene greed and stupidity of the current system. They recognize that we are rapidly destroying ourselves along with our world. Those who retain some consciousness of higher values are generally in despair. They cannot understand that the end foreshadows a new beginning. Yet, it is the very loss of hope that is forcing humans to turn inward again, to drop all our façades and re-discover what is real in us. Few can yet see around the bend of time to the coming global emergence of our long-repressed higher consciousness. But, thankfully, we are closer to that renewal than ever. Our suffering will soon be transmuted back into original bliss.

Even as the old and terminally ill system crumbles, the human spirit is about to brighten, to learn to shine with a clearer light than we can possibly conceptualize. We are at the dawn of a new era of emancipation from the pathologies of egocentricity. Ironically, at the moment when the dominant scientistic ideology has convinced most of us that God is just a fairy tale, we are about to encounter the power of our Supreme Being in the most dramatic way possible.

Until one has re-discovered original bliss, one is doomed to a life of anguish. This is important to recognize, so that one can put one's priorities straight. As a well-known sacred text advises, "First seek ye the kingdom of heaven; then all things shall be added unto thee."

Don't seek the limited kingdoms first—the conquest of sexual partners, money, fame, profession, status, children, etc.—or you will waste your life in hysteria, angst, obsession, aggression, insecurity, and dissatisfaction.

First realize the blissful Self, and then your path in life will be clear and effortless. On the worldly level, we all have our special gifts and our intrinsic capacities, but they are usually bound up with neurotic tendencies, or rendered inoperative because of overwhelming psychological complexes that paralyze us and prevent us from blossoming into the fullness of our potentialities. Once we have realized the rapturous awareness of the Supreme Self, all our creative capacities will flow into life spontaneously. Situations will unfold naturally in which we create loving connections with others who recognize and appreciate who we are and what we have to offer.

The ego is like the disciple Thomas, who asked Jesus: When will the kingdom of heaven come? Jesus the Yogi answered: The Kingdom is here now, but you do not see it.

When you regain your original blissful awareness, the world indeed will be perceived as heavenly—even though our heaven is currently going through a period of hell. Only by perceiving in a heavenly way, making our heaven manifest again through the power of liberated awareness, can we restore the lost paradise conditions to this phenomenal realm. This world is only a dream of our collective consciousness within the greater Dream of God. We hold the keys to the secrets of Nature within us, but our egoic illusions prevent us from using them. It is a wondrous paradox indeed.

Blissful awareness, our true essence, is supernatural and super-intelligent, with powers far beyond anything the limited mental capacities of the ego can imagine. This is because our true being is the Being of the universe itself, the Supreme Being who created this universe, the underlying reality of all that is, and infinitely more than all that appears.

Once we realize our true relationship with Supreme Beingness, the Heart will open and divine love will flow. It is this inconceivably pure love that is the substance of our bliss.

The love we have for the Self, for God, is the love God has for us. This love is our sustenance. It is the source of strength, of wisdom, and of hope. Have faith in this immovable Rock of the ages. Love is the foundation of what makes us human—and potentially divine. Rest in the original bliss that is God's loving embrace. We are permeated with the sweet essence of the Divine Presence. Once we open to that ultimate blessing, all other blessings will follow.

The Virtue of Subtlety

Spiritual development can be conceived as the attainment of increasingly subtle levels of Being.

Subtlety itself is a concept too subtle for our mainstream gross, materialistic, scientistic paradigm to understand. Physics grasps the extraordinary nature of the extremely large and the extremely small. The laws of physics applicable at normal size ranges deform, become more and more surreal, at both the level of enormous celestial bodies and at the level of subatomic particles, even to the point of science having to accept that particles morph into probability waves, being indeterminable and unlocalizable.

On the mental slope of reality, the field of psychoanalysis is aware of at least some of the subtleties of our psychodynamics, the complexes and agencies that function in unconscious strata of the egoic mind, producing such enigmas as parapraxes, synchronicities, paranormal phenomena, and psychosomatic events.

Chinese medicine, working also on the subtle side, manipulates the pranic energy that flows through the meridians of the physical organism and maintains its bio-electromagnetic field. Homeopathy works with extremely minute dilutions of substances—and some would say, with the manipulation of signifiers and the placebo effect. But that is about the limit of subtlety in most fields of scientific research.

In the field of philosophy, the story is similar. Anglo-American philosophy focuses on subtleties of logic and critical thinking, including the paradoxes of self-referentiality. But it does not break through the box of objective reality. Continental European philosophy in such forms as phenomenology and poststructuralism goes to a deeper level of subtlety, focusing on the fractured, unstable, representational, and parallactic nature of subjectivity—but it still ties itself securely to the Cartesian subject of the senses, of affects, of language, and of history.

Only in the most rarified Eastern pursuits of the truth of our Being, in Yogic traditions ranging from Advaita to Zen, and in the esoteric mystical lineages of the West and Middle East that came originally from the same sources, does subtlety reach the level of our essence. It is in these Yogic traditions that the subtlest kernel of the Self is recognized. By virtue of focusing on the extremely subtle vibrations of pure consciousness, in states of deep meditation, one accesses the fundament of Being. By emptying the mind of all thought contents, Yogis achieve the most subtle empirical realization of all—that of absolute nothingness, the immanent-yet-transcendent Ground of pure awareness.

This, the sweetest fruit of meditative stillness, yields the understanding that nothingness and somethingness are two aspects of a single whole. There are profound consequences to this realization. The impact of the recognition that 'I am nothing, absolutely nothing, the nothing that contains the entire universe, time, and all forms in motion' resonates through the psyche, ripples through the organism, and alters the vibrational matrix that forms the universe itself. The cosmic dream awakens to its dreamer.

Nothingness is the source of everything. When awareness settles into absolute nothingness, its transfinite potentiality appears as the primal quantum wave. This omnipresent wave of noumenal presence vibrates as and beyond space and time, as eternal rapture, inconceivably awesome intelligence, and divine love. The wave potential coalesces into cosmic world-dreams of pure delight.

At the inter-subjective level, within the field of space-time, the wave potential continues to flow into reality with pulsations of compassion, wisdom, and joy. On the individual level, the vibratory resonance of nothingness dissolves all identifications, emerging as the clear light of cosmic consciousness, eternal now-ness, and freedom from fear and negativity. Silent presence aware as egoic absence embraces all beings as manifestations of the One Self, the Transfinite Zero.

Wondrous laughter resounds at the far side of this realization, which is simultaneously the near side of illusion, closer than the world itself, perceived as a bubble in the infinite sea of potentiality that is the mind of God. This is the way the world ends: not with a bang, nor a whimper, but with a cosmic laugh of incomprehensible comprehension.

The scientific model of causality is, as Hume observed, only the narrative fantasy of the collective ego. Historicism is an excuse for resentment and hatred. We blame our suffering on parents, siblings, society, other cultures, races, nations, religions, and genders. If only we can eliminate all our enemies, our Others, or at least get them to grovel at our feet, we believe we shall be avenged. The dirty fantasy of every ego spills its toxic waste into the planetary dreamfield, converting our world into a nightmarish wasteland.

There is a way to overcome all this. It is a very subtle way, one that will not appeal to many. But then, not many are needed to pull it off. The secret of power lies not in numbers, money, or explosive devices—but in subtlety. When we are no longer invested in gross existence, nor in its urgencies, its drives for pleasure, when the locus of life is discovered in the most subtle dimension beyond both the biological and psychological realms, all anxieties drop away. An understanding is about to emerge, in what is quaintly referred to as real time, which will soon confound the people of the world. The logic of super-organismic unity will (super)naturally replace the logic of the warring multitudes. The Self, liberated from ego, will restore the latent oneness of all beings into a unified expression of our Being. A single cosmic intelligence will animate and coordinate all beings. Harmony will be restored to planetary existence.

This is truly how the world ends: with a new beginning, and the laughter of the Rapture.

As consciousness becomes progressively subtler, through meditative practice, what had been accepted as normal life is recognized as a kind of death, the imaginary existence of an entity that never was. And from that subtler perspective, in the symbolic realm of higher meaning, what had previously been looked upon not only as the end of human civilization, but as a horrid failure of intelligence and cooperation, will be perceived as the necessary pre-condition of the new beginning.

The ironic fate of the human ego, bringing about its own collective destruction out of the conceit of its godlike ability to act in any damn way it pleases, regardless of the effect upon Nature, is its collapse into victim-hood, blaming God (or chance) for the results of its own wanton malpractice of existence. The shattering of this demiurgic entity, the fall of its evil masquerade through the parade of history, heralds planetary re-awakening to the almighty power the world's great spiritual teachers have always served.

Maintaining the ego is a luxury we can no longer afford. Those who play around in the dirty pools of the lower vibrations, indulging in greed, envy, anger, lust, and irresponsible inertia, are discovering that there is a limit to what the universe will allow before lowering the boom. We have reached the end of our margin of error: Living viciously and in bad faith is not sustainable. We are reaping the whirlwind. Every ego is now on the verge of cracking up—or else it has already. The end is nearer than most would like to think.

Only a very subtle and interiorized intelligence, one that is truthful and reverent, devoted to the service of the Most Subtle, open to the inflow of the most exalted energies and information, will have the wherewithal to cross the tightrope from the imminent end to the immanent beginning. To gain the virtue of such subtlety, only complete surrender of the mind, the will, and the heart to our Supreme Being will suffice. This is all that lies within our power—and yet it is enough.

The Transfiguration of Ishtar

Easter is the most important day in the Christian calendar. Yet the word Easter does not appear in the Bible. Easter is simply a misspelling of the name Ishtar, the Goddess of Babylon (now known as Iraq). It is more than coincidental that at this late hour of Kali Yuga, Christendom should return to Babylon, albeit unconsciously, to confront its own spiritual roots. Some would even say Ishtar has been crucified by Christendom, and now is rising up once again.

The Goddess Ishtar long predated both Hebrew and Christian theologies. She is the ultimate goddess, of dense and many-layered symbolism, and her influence reaches secretly across the globe. Let us try to put together the puzzle Ishtar represents.

First, of course, we must refer to the obvious patriarchalization of religious imagery that led to the aphanisis of the goddess from Christian dogma. Much later in history, the feminine element slips back into Catholic theology, with the official ascension of Mary. But otherwise, the influence of Ishtar remains only in such traces as the giving of her name to the holiest day in the Christian calendar.

In one of the basic mythic narratives, Ishtar, the Queen of Heaven, travels to the underworld. At each of its Seven Gates, she has to remove one part of her attire, starting with her crown. As she does this, she loses more and more of her power.

She is eventually captured by the evil goddess of the underworld, Erish-Kegal. She ends up naked and bleeding, draped over a tree. The Father God, Anu, works to rescue Ishtar by fashioning two Elementals, the Water of Life and the Clay of Life. The two

Elementals cleverly work their way down through the Seven Gates, and sprinkle the Water and Clay of Life upon Ishtar. This enables her to climb back up the seven rungs of the Ladder of Light, retrieving her attire and her power, to become Queen of Heaven once again.

One can easily perceive in this narrative the structure of the chakras of Kundalini Yoga and their attendant assemblage points. In brief, our infinite consciousness has descended from its fullness of light and wisdom down to the lowest, most neurotic and psychotic, levels of ego.

The image of being naked and bleeding, draped over a tree, is of course analogous to the image of Christ on the cross. The water of life is also familiar to Christian mythology, in the rite of baptism. The combination of water and clay refers to a fundamental principle of the ancient Shiite science of *al-kimia*, known in the West as alchemy. The principle is known famously in Latin as "*Solve et Coagula.*" This refers to the capacity to dissolve, or de-crystallize, the ego structure and coagulate, or re-crystallize it, at a higher assemblage point, a higher frequency and level of coherence.

Ishtar's losing of her clothing and her crown on the downward path into the hell realm of ego-consciousness, and her regaining of that attire on the upward journey, is still memorialized in the old Christian custom of wearing something new on Easter. A new garment worn on this day would bring good luck through the coming year. The birds would punish those who wore old attire by dropping 'decorations' on them from the air. In fact, the Easter Parade grew out of the old beliefs about dressing up in new clothing. This grand event provided a chance to be seen wearing the latest fashions. The elegant ritual unfortunately also reinforced social hierarchies through conspicuous displays of wealth.

Of course, all that is simply an egoic distortion of the true meaning of the clothes. They represent the virtues and capacities of consciousness (in Yogic terms, these are called *siddhis*) that are gained as the lower drives and emotions are sublimated on the inner journey of Self-realization.

In a second, dualist version of the myth, Ishtar went to the underworld to rescue her son-lover Tammuz. The descent into Hell took three days. During this time there was sterility and a suspension of sexual activities over the whole earth. It culminated in the Day of Joy, when Tammuz was returned to life, which began the New Year.

The Christ myth can be seen clearly here. Even Christ's three-day journey into Hell was taken from this mytheme. Of course, we should understand it to refer to the Hell of the unconscious mind of the ego. By descending into our own inner Hell and rescuing the lost spark of consciousness trapped down there, we may accomplish the great task of redeeming ourselves from unconsciousness, and attaining re-divinization.

The Day of Joy refers to the moment when this re-divinization has occurred planet-wide, ushering in an era Yogis call Sat Yuga, a new Golden Age. We can also see in this structure the paradigm of spiritual renunciation, in which penitents take vows of chastity, until they no longer identify with body or name and their energy of desire has been raised from an obsession with sex to a one-pointed desire for union with the Supreme Being.

Ishtar is the goddess of many names. She is also known as Astarte. The word "star" derives from her name, and she is said to be an actual star, sometimes Sirius and other times Venus. In her form of Morning Star, she is the goddess of war and carnage, and as the Evening Star, the goddess of love and bliss. In other words, her coming represents the moment of transition between Kali Yuga and Sat Yuga. As such, she is also the goddess who brings peace, and in that capacity has been called Semiramis (the one who holds the olive branch, in other words, the dove) and later the Roman deity Columba, goddess of the New World. In early Semitic myths, she is referred to as Adon, the Lord, which evolved into Athon, and in

Greek became both Adonis and Athena. In Christianity, of course, she was trans-signified from Adon to Madonna.

In Hebrew mythology, she is the Shekhinah, the Holy Spirit. She is also the "beloved" of the Song of Songs, and is on the one hand the harlot of the gods (the "hierodule of heaven," Belit, the Black One, known as Kali in India), but on the other hand she is the mother and virgin. She is spoken of as the "virgin womb of Chaos." In pre-Hebrew Canaanite mythology, her icon is the Tree, and her name is Asherah. In Assyria, she becomes Inanna, and later Estera, and is re-introduced into Jewish mythology as Queen Esther. In Norse mythology, she is called Freya, and is the goddess celebrated on Good Friday.

We could go on a long time naming all her avatars in every culture, from the German goddess Hertha to the Chinese Heavenly Queen Shing Mu. You can find her everywhere. Moreover, this most shape-shifting goddess is present in a different form at every level of consciousness. In fact, she is the earliest representation of the Supreme Being in all the modifications, crystallizations, expansions and contractions of Being from the Absolute to matter to the finite egoic persona.

Babylonian scriptures called her the Light of the World, Lord and Leader of Hosts, Opener of the Womb, Righteous Judge, Lawgiver, Goddess of Goddesses, Bestower of Strength, Framer of All Decrees, Lady of Victory, and Forgiver of Sins. Much of the liturgical flattery addressed to God in the Old Testament was taken directly from Babylonian prayers to Ishtar.

At the highest level, that of Chakra Seven, Ishtar is the Great Nothingness, the Void, the womb of the All, and is referred to as Ashura. In India, this state of transfinite potency is referred to as Brahman. She is also known as the Goddess of the Gaze, and is pictured as the All-Seeing Eye at the top of the pyramid that represents in freemasonry the descent of Spirit into the world.

At Chakra Six, she is the lover of God. In India, at this level she is known as Ishi and her divine lover is Ishwara. In another tradition, the same couple is referred to as Shakti and Shiva. She is the radiant light of the Star of Luminous Awareness. In Egypt, of course, she is famous as Isis, and she descends to recover the scattered pieces of the body of her divine lover, Osiris. In Tibet, Ishtar shortened her name to Tara, and she took on yet other names in China and Japan, yet always the Queen of Heaven and the Lady (Madonna) of the Great Lord. She is also, among other titles, the goddess of the Sun.

As she descends to Chakra Five, she enters the Cosmic Egg, the archetypal origin of all form, from which she will be reborn into the Earthly plane. Here she takes the name Sophia, and is renowned as the goddess of wisdom. And of course the egg symbolism has remained with us in the form of the Easter egg. Her name Estera later took on the meaning of estrus (ovulation) and is present in the hormone Estrogen. In Latin countries, she has evolved into the piñata, which is often made in the form of a star. It is whacked open (an allusion not only to the opening of the womb—and the heart—but to the higher purposes of karmic suffering, and the rites of dharma combat) to reveal its treasures.

At Chakra Four, she incarnates as both Athena and Aphrodite. She is the union of divine love and law. In Egypt, she also gives birth to Time (her son/lover is named Horus, from whom we have the hours). In Greece, she can also be recognized in the myth of Persephone, the beautiful virgin goddess who is ravished by Hades, the lord of Hell, yet who remains a virgin ("thou still unravished bride of Time"), and thereafter spends half her life in the underworld and half in the upper regions with her mother, Demeter. This myth, of course refers to the soul's wandering between truth and illusion, nirvana and samsara, from noumenon to phenomenon, as well as the journey through Time from Sat Yuga to Kali Yuga and back again. She can be seen in yet another form in the Indian epic *Ramayana* as Sita, the pure wife of the warrior god

Rama. She is abducted by the great demon Ravana and rescued with the help of the divine monkey Hanuman. In other words, human nature oscillates between sublime and bestial, the soul belongs to God part of the time and to the Devil the other part.

When she enters the lower levels of the labyrinth, her star changes. She is no longer Venus, the goddess of divine love, but Sirius, the Dog Star. She becomes the estrus, and, as with a bitch in heat, she drives the male dogs into a frenzy. This berserk bestiality, in the form of the quest to be top dog, is the goal of Chakra Three. In Chakra Two, she becomes the sexual drive itself, the Whore of Babylon, and in Chakra One she enters the frozen form of total inertia and unconsciousness, the womb of Death.

The entire play of consciousness is revealed in the archetypal imagery of Ishtar. She has now completed her descent. The Cosmic Dream has reached its final stop, the lowest, frozen depths of Hell. Now is the moment of Ishtar's rise. In Chakra One, she morphs into the Kundalini serpent, the energy of Self-awareness that rises through all the chakras, breaking through the seven Veils of Maya to regain the majesty of pure Spirit.

Ishtar is not just a myth, nor is she someone else, who lived long ago. Ishtar is your Self. This myth is your story, an awesome and miraculous dream that is about to unfold in ways you never imagined.

Some Implications of Ego Death

There is a common misunderstanding concerning the implications of ego death. Many people assume that, once the ego dies in the process of spiritual transcendence, the individual can have no further will to live. This is incorrect. The will to live actually becomes more powerful than ever. But now it is a wholocentric will, rather than that of an imaginary, body-identified, fragmented subject. The Self whose will comes to function through the mind, now employs the organism for higher purposes that serve the Whole.

After the death of the ego, there is a rebirth. This is why the process has been referred to with such metaphors as that of the snake shedding its skin, the moon shedding its shadow, and the caterpillar becoming a butterfly. Rather than bringing about a lack of will to live, which is often how the ego feels—indeed many egos have a wish not to live, if not an active suicidal drive—the reborn Self will be filled with joyous energy, fully empowered, liberated from the weight of negative emotions, flying in the upper reaches of angelic intelligence, engaged in creative projects for the well-being and salvation of our besieged planet.

Those who imagine that ego death means sitting around aimlessly in a state of blankness do not recognize the creative intelligence of the Supreme Being. Once the ego surrenders to the Absolute Intelligence and Power of the Self, life really begins. What dies is the bundle of egoic attributes that usually include confusion, apathy, aggressivity, anxiety, misery, and other forms of narcissistic pettiness.

After ego surrenders to Self, or God (or in Buddhist discourse, after one realizes the truth of Emptiness), one accepts life in its suchness and acts effortlessly in pure love, serenity, and intuitive clarity—with a boundless, selfless appetite for service, for being an instrument of salvation for all beings. In the Buddhist tradition, this is known as functioning as a Bodhisattva. In the Hindu tradition, one arrived at this ultimate stage of spiritual development is considered a jivan mukta, liberated while alive.

There is no feeling of deadness in one who has passed through the sacred process of ego death and rebirth, but an exquisite aliveness that the ego cannot understand. This is because the ego is a fictional tissue of identifications designed and installed with the purpose of adapting to others, getting approval, manipulating people and situations, gaining power over others, and indulging in such pathological pleasures as revenge, debasement, and even destruction of those who are perceived as enemies. These unpleasant aspects of the human ego are what require its death and rebirth.

Of course, some egos are healthier than others. Some egos function as pillars of society and use their powers mostly for good. They may be quite ethical, appreciative of higher values, of beauty, of the importance of taking care of the natural environment, and they may even be religious. What is the difference between a good ego that functions in a highly principled, idealistic, and adaptive manner, and one who has undergone ego death and rebirth?

The difference can be understood only if one grasps the structure of the ego. The ego is split. Its will is not single, whole, and integrated, but multiple, dispersed, fractured; and its word-filled mind is utterly uncontrollable by its own conscious center. Neither does the conscious subject know what is actually going on in its own subconscious regions.

The conscious part of the ego is thus not in control of the ego's covert agendas. The conscious part of the ego is usually not even aware of the axioms, phantasies, traces of traumas, oedipal wishes, and superego commands that operate constantly from below the horizon of the cognitive and conative jurisdiction of the consciousness. That is why the ego can be said to be in a condition of false consciousness. Even when that false consciousness functions for the ostensible betterment of the world, it is operating within a larger command system that limits, and often countermands, its effectiveness. Moreover, the unconscious operating system yields such poisonous fruits as anxiety and other negative emotional residues, such that one is generally in a state of suffering, and never in rapture.

The ego may know exceptional moments of happiness, but they are usually situation-governed. One may, for example, transcend the ego during peak experiences, perhaps moments in beautiful natural settings, like watching a sunset on a beach, or while running a marathon, or ingesting drugs or alcohol, or while involved in sexual intercourse. But these will not last, and some will have negative consequences. The joy of Being eludes even the most principled and idealistic egoic identity. The push-and-pull of its attachments and fears is always sabotaging its ability to be present and serene.

The death of the ego means the death of deadness; the death of suffering; the death of moral, psychological, aesthetic, and spiritual blindness; the death of fear and enmeshment. The death of ego implies oneness with LIFE.

Of course, bringing about the demise of the ego is not usually an easy matter. That is why the science of Sat Yoga has developed a battery of techniques to help achieve this end. Through the increase of awareness and understanding, the disabling of outmoded defense mechanisms, and the lifting of repressions, comes the increase of *shakti*—those glowing flows of spiritual energy that are transmitted from the Source, both directly and via illumined teachers and communities of compassionate, evolving souls. Through wholehearted discipleship and devoted practice, the grace of egoless presence will manifest as the mindful miracle of Being.

As the Bible asks us, what good is it to gain the whole world if in the process you lose your soul? The ego is the very condition of soul loss. The death of the ego is the regaining of soul—in fact of the divine spirit that transcends even the realm of soul—and the gateway to reunion with the Absolute.

Only if enough of us apparent human entities are willing to achieve the inner transformation that will re-make us as manifestations of the One Without a Second will our planetary home have a second chance to flourish as a Paradise. Let us take refuge in the Heart, the One Self, and create a world of harmonious community. We can learn to live together once more in the grace of Presence, in wise innocence and profound playfulness. This is our highest calling and our true destiny. May our clashing profane egos die that our unity-in-divinity may live again!

Becoming Marjiva

People often ask what is the best way to meditate. There are, of course, many techniques—from counting breaths to subvocal repetition of a mantra to staring at a candle flame—but the only true way to meditate is to die.

Of course, biological death is not what is referred to, but death of the ego with its narcissistic, chattering mind. To die while alive is the universal method of spiritual transfiguration. Learning to die was considered the essence of philosophy by no less an exponent than Socrates.

Becoming dead as an ego is the method espoused by such great figures in world spirituality as Shankara, Buddha, Lao Tzu, Christ, and Muhammad, and by such well-known sages in their various traditions as Meister Eckhart, Ibn Arabi, Rumi, Ramana Maharshi, and Dogen Zenji. It can be truly said that this is the one universal religion.

To die to the ego and be reborn as the cosmic Self—this is the one attainment that unites all spiritual paths.

To be dead while alive—in Sanskrit, the term for this ecstatic state of Being is *Marjiva*—means that the mind has stopped dancing around, hopping from past to future, from happiness to sadness, from love to hate. Power struggles come to an end. No further narratives are composed in the mind. When the mind dies into simple, wise presence, life truly begins.

How is this pure state of Being to be reached? It can be gradual or sudden. Even when it is sudden, though, there must have been a period of preparation in order for the soul to be ripe for Self-realization. Yet, in fact, the state is not reached or constructed, but simply realized. You are already simple presence. The obscuring clouds of thought and emotion just have to dissolve for you to know that.

Spiritual practice is the process of dissolving those clouds. Along the way, there is a ripening of the soul, a deepening, transmuting and transfiguring of the ego structure, little by little, to let in more light, more serenity, more time in simple presence. The inner work can also be seen as a channeling of energies, a maturation of the soul's inherent potentials. It involves a reconfiguration of defense mechanisms, exchanging such tendencies as aggression, inertia, deception, and avoidance, for such noble qualities as tolerance, wisdom, compassion, generosity, and courage. These attributes are natural to the Real Self, but can only fully emerge with the death of the false self.

The false self dwells in duality. There are internal splits—between inner child and superego, good and bad, past and future, et cetera—that prevent the ego mind from perceiving reality as it is. Models of relationship from the past are projected on the present and thus turn the future into a repetition of the past; value systems are employed for purposes of gaining judgmental superiority; and situations are manipulated to create scenarios of victimhood, in which self-righteous anger and revenge are justified.

All this is done to keep from having to do the one thing the ego must refrain from doing in order to maintain its illusory existence: love.

To die while alive means to live in love. It means to forgive unconditionally. It means to let go of the past. It means to surrender utterly and forever—mind and body, thoughts, words, and actions—to the All-Encompassing Power that is the creative force behind, within, and beyond both the soul and the universe. This power manifests as All, as Emptiness, and as the Self. The cosmic consciousness can be felt as the vibratory energy of which both mind and matter are made: Awareness, Love, and Light.

To die into the supernal Light, like the proverbial moth flying into the Flame—this is the one true act that we can perform. Once the ego has been burned up in the Sacrificial Fire of pure Love, time morphs into eternity. Body and awareness continue to function, but without the illusion of an egoic agency.

A silent mind that is fully present, light-hearted, loving, intuitive, charitable, stable and dependable, replaces the now-dead flighty moth-mind of the ego.

Life becomes a field of grace. In Buddhism, it is called Sukhavati, the place of bliss.

Once the ego is dead, every moment becomes miraculous. Freed from the struggle between loss and gain, underdog and top dog, all events are experienced as blessings.

We are all being led to this state of beatitude, but some of us will only get there kicking and screaming, as a result of unbearable suffering. Every day, all of us die a little. We are killed by the disappointments we are dealt by other egos, by the betrayals of loved ones, the losses of attachment figures, the corruption and fall of role models, the break-up of partnerships, the family battles that erupt over inheritances, and other issues.

Every day, we learn more how the war clouds are darkening, the dead are piling up, the blood of whole nations is flowing, the ecological web of life is being destroyed, the glaciers are melting and the seas are rising; we feel the seismic shaking, the monster storms, the tsunamis gathering, the bombs exploding.

We know that our civilization is at an end. It is destined to fall, to be stricken by a long series of ever worsening catastrophes. All this has already been set in motion by the collective ego. We know our current inadequate organization of consciousness must die, if life is to survive. A new, higher civilization must rise Phoenix-like from the ruins, a new community based on unity and divine love.

To kill one's ego now is imperative for all of us, it is the urgent command of God. All the prophets of every land and time have shouted this message down the defiles of history. But now is the moment of apocalyptic revelation.

It is time to put away childish things. Let us become very serious about what we are doing to the Earth. Let the healing begin. It requires our conscious premeditated ego-death and our sacred theomorphic rebirth.

All blessings for becoming Marjiva.

The Supreme Liberation

S at Yoga is a path for the courageous, for those willing to train unremittingly to become impeccable spiritual warriors, those who dedicate their lives to transforming themselves into egoless embodiments of goodness, love, creative wisdom, joy, and spiritual power. Sat Yoga is a samurai dharma, for those who, like Buddha facing the three temptations, or Arjuna in the *Bhagavad Gita*, in union with God enter fully into the battle against ignorance, lust, anger, illusion, and the full onslaught of the egoic realm. The path of Sat Yoga leads those who are victorious to the Supreme Liberation.

Liberation while the body remains alive, the state known as *Jivan Mukti*, is not liberation *from* life, but liberation *into* life. It signifies release from enslavement to false principles and powers, and the attainment of the freedom to manifest the fullness of our spiritual potency in serene and joyous creativity. It signifies the liberation of our divine nature to claim its rightful dominion over the illusions of the phenomenal realm. It implies ultimately the liberation not simply of an individual, but of our whole species, in fact our planet, from usurpation by the demonic forces of the dominant collective ego-system.

Along the way toward the Supreme Liberation, a number of different levels of partial liberation will be achieved. The first liberation to occur for many is liberation from the most primitive affects and drives of the ego: freedom from paranoia, anxiety, and depression; and from addictive, sociopathic, psychopathic or psychotic propensities; and from even the least taint of aggressivity, obsessiveness, timidity, confusion, and despair. All the ways that invasive thoughts can cause suffering are alleviated by the natural mind-control offered by the practice of Sat Yoga.

Essentially, all liberation is freedom from the egoic mind—the false consciousness that views the world through a petty, distorted, narcissistic lens. The egocentric mind is not only mired in delusion, but is fragmented and in a constant war among its own constituent identifications and fantasies. The bulk of the ego lies unperceived beneath the threshold of consciousness, so that the small part that is conscious mistakes itself for the whole, which is the cause of all that is most dark and ridiculous in the human comedy.

The conscious part of the ego rationalizes its behavior, but the real agent that pulls the strings remains hidden, censoring the conscious mind's access to the information that could lead to liberation from its enslavement to unconscious urges, prohibitions, refusals, assumptions, axioms, phantasms, buried traumatic memories, misplaced loyalties, forbidden and unbearable re-cognitions. This pathological mode of operation in Yogic terminology is called *avidya*, ignorance. Consciousness is caught and dismembered by the three-headed dog of hell (called Cerberus among the Greeks) representing the lower passions. In Buddhism, they are known as the passion of ignorance (*moha*), the passion of greedy desire (*raga*), and the passion of hatred and revenge (*dvesha*).

The way to break out of this hell is to learn to use the mind in new ways. Becoming adept in the higher capacities of our symbolic intelligence can be accelerated with the help of a skilled psycho-spiritual guide. In the Yogic schema, the conscious egoic mind has three elements: *manas, ahankar,* and *buddhi.* The latter two can be considered as centers, or attractors, while the first is the flow of signifiers (words and images), carried on waves of affect, moving constantly between them. *Ahankar* refers to the demanding narcissistic sense of 'me, me, me.'

Before one enters the spiritual process, the flow of the *manas* revolves almost entirely around the 'me'. There is a ceaseless emission of banal signifiers in the conscious adult mind operating according to the pleasure principle—while the unconscious mind is an infantile ego enmeshed in conflictive scenarios with internalized others, scenarios that produce symptoms in both body and mind. While this is going on, these scenarios are also being projected outward, creating the resistance of apparently external reality.

The first step in inner work is to redirect the flow of *manas* toward the higher center, the *buddhi*, the intellect proper, which is impersonal and therefore more lucid, retaining the capacity for detached evaluation. This redirection of the mind requires *ab initio* a new set of values that affirm the primacy of *buddhi* over *ahankar*, of symbolic intelligence over egoic enjoyment. Such self-re-education is what is referred to as the inculcation of *gyana*, the higher knowledge of the Self.

But *gyana* can too easily become deformed into a parrot-like repetition of mantras or abstract concepts that carry no weight against the more visceral urges and pleasures offered by *ahankar*. What usually happens is that consciousness fractures further, with the addition of a "spiritual" subpersonality, an illusory image of transcendence, while the old egoic patterns and pleasures are maintained behind the façade.

For a true breakthrough to occur, the dynamic energy of *manas* flowing toward *buddhi* must become strong enough to activate its latent powers. This involves creating a link between *buddhi* and *Atman*. The symbolic meaning-making capacity must surrender to the Holy Spirit. This act converts *gyana* into *vigyana*—knowledge becomes wisdom.

Vigyana is a powerful antidote to the surreptitious sabotage of *ahankar*. *Vigyana* is the acid of discernment that eats through the egoic veneer of denial. It is not analysis in the usual sense thought of by the ego, which is just strategic gaming, but a higher power of spirit that is activated by *Karuna*, divine love. Through Being-love, consciousness can break through all resistances and dead-end paths of the imaginary matrix.

The wisdom activity of the *buddhi* develops into a strong energy field within the psyche (this is what is referred to as soul-consciousness). This attracts archetypal concepts and *sattvic* openings into *kairos*, the trans-egoic vertical dimension of time, which become explosive weapons for the spiritual warrior to defeat the *rajasic* (hyperactive) onslaughts of the lower passions and the *tamasic* (inert) lethargy of deadened, cynical thought-forms. Wisdom, once activated in the *buddhi*, becomes a permanent presence, an internalized, empowered *Atman*-analyst, deconstructing all the veils of Maya from within. This attainment greatly accelerates the process of spiritual purification.

Eventually, however, the *vigyana* process itself becomes an obstacle, and it must also be deconstructed. This requires the activation of a yet higher power of Divine Intelligence, called *pragya paramita*, or ultimate transcendental wisdom, which emerges not from *buddhi*, but directly from *Atman*. The power of silence, emptiness, called *Shunyata*, is then apperceived as the all-encompassing open and boundless space of pure awareness.

Vigyana is a psychic antibody that works to overpower the poison of dualistic thought, misperception, and flawed action. But *vigyana* is itself embedded in dualistic thought, although at a higher level of archetypal understanding, since it is part of the operation of the *Logos* in its pure form. It results in pristine concepts and realizations that point to the truth of nonduality, but it does not reach the Real of nonduality. It remains an emergent property of the symbolic order, and just like Moses, cannot enter the Promised Land that lies beyond the symbolizing intellect.

However, when *vigyana* has completed its sacred work, it dissolves into a single point of infinitely condensed attention. This produces the state known as *nirvikalpa samadhi*—complete absorption in the dimension beyond thought. It is then that the all-unifying light of *Atman* is revealed. Thus begins the celebration of the holy matrimony of Being and Becoming, Time and Eternity, the One and the Many, Noumenon and Phenomenon. There is no longer a knower separate from the known. Of course, there never was—there was never anyone needing to be liberated—that was part of the illusion. There is no analyst and no thoughts to be analyzed. All is Suchness (*tathata*). There are no discrete objects. Every apparent being penetrates every other. All is a single Whole. Time itself is eternity.

The realization of the Absolute, *Parabrahman*, enables the final step of the path to be taken—full embodiment of the Supreme Being in *avataric* presence functioning for the liberation of our planetary reality.

This is the next step in our evolution. Many people around the globe are taking this step now, even without knowing that others are on the same path. It is no mere coincidence, but rather an ordained synchronicity that this step is being taken just as our world is entering the deepest darkness and destructiveness in history, a cultural collapse of unprecedented magnitude. Necessity is indeed the mother of evolutionary leaps. The current conditions are increasing the impetus to achieve our transformational imperative.

There is no other way out. We must all come to realize the Supreme Self behind the petty ego. In the final surrender of the limited identity to the unlimited, more and more human beings are coming to live no longer as separate egos, but, tearing down the wall of illusion, to function as facets of the one all-encompassing, all-permeating, cosmic Diamond. We are learning to live as a single planetary super-organism.

We are the universe, a single Whole of self-luminous awareness, divine at every level, from the subatomic to the molecular to the celestial, through all forms of matter, life, mind, soul, and spirit. We are once more learning to re-dream reality with the power of awakened Mind. We shall once more live as gods on our paradise planet, co-dreamers of the glorious dream emerging in the Cosmic Mind. We are here to create such a perfect world now, and to enjoy our incomparable achievement for ages to come. And all the while, we are the perfect stillness of eternal Presence. Every illusion is falling away. We are nearing the hour of our Supreme Liberation.

EPILOGUE

Seven Endnotes to the Endless

Seven Endnotes to the Endless

Regardless of where you may be in your spiritual journey, or what demons remain to be slain, there are seven bits of timeless advice that have been found to be of priceless value. They have been discovered and shared by all true spiritual teachers since time immemorial. The first is: Be fearless. There is nothing to fear because you are immortal, eternal, imperishable Being. You are formless intelligence, part of the supreme intelligence that formed the Cosmos. Simply through the act of disidentification from the bodily vehicle, fearlessness is easily achieved.

The second bit of advice offered by every spiritual tradition is: Be at peace. Trust that everything that happens is part of a higher plan and is leading to the best possible ultimate result. Act without concern for results, but only with the most benevolent intentions, the most skillful means available, and the fullest and most caring attention. Leave the outcome in the hands of God. This will bring peace and serenity. When you accept the past as well as the future with unconditional forgiveness and trust, your serenity will be complete and absolute.

The third item of advice: Be in love. Love life, love even more the Creator of life, realize the miracle that all this is. Be constantly astonished at the wonders all around you. Every blade of grass, every birdsong, every sunset is a manifestation of Cosmic Being, an explosion of Divine Love. Even the most aversive people and situations are here to teach you essential lessons, to show you your own unconscious projections, to motivate you to gain greater wisdom and spiritual power. You are part of it all, and from another perspective, it is all here for your appreciation. Enjoy the marvels of the Real and feel the love with which they have been created and offered to you. Love is both energy and matter—and Love is all that matters.

Fourth: Be the light. You are in fact the light of the world. Your consciousness is light. Your light illumines others. Keep your mind radiant. Don't obscure the light with dark thoughts or feelings. Remain the witness of all that happens, detached, discerning, clear and luminous. Light is your essential nature, and the nature of the Universe as well.

Fifth, remember your Source continually, and you will be naturally desireless. You will feel profoundly that you have within you everything you need. The body will eat when it is truly hungry, and it will choose healthy food in the right amount. But there will be no drive to overeat. And if sometime there is no food to eat, the body will cope with that, without suffering. There will be no addictions or compulsions to ingest any substances or to engage in any activities or possess any objects of pleasure that are not appropriate, natural, and wholesome. Greed will vanish. Generosity will emerge. Dispassion will remain constant. Relationships of the highest kind will effortlessly flourish. A cheerful disposition, healing laughter, and deep spiritual friendship will be revealed as the greatest treasures of existence.

Sixth, through remaining centered in silent awareness, you will achieve true empowerment. You will receive the power of Spirit to remain unmoved in the face of both temptation and terror. You will be able to transmit the power of healing energy to others. You will radiate an aura of strength in which others can take refuge. You will have the perseverance to fulfill your life's mission. You will have, when the time comes, the power to die joyously, as you have lived.

Seventh, through perfect surrender to the Supreme Self, you will achieve Emptiness. Be empty now: empty yourself of egocentric concerns and distractions. Empty the mind of mundane thoughts.

Open your heart to boundless love. Let your emptiness become so vast it encompasses the entire Universe. Realize you are one with God. In the Emptiness that is the Absolute, overwhelming Fullness gives birth to new worlds, even as old ones die and disappear. The Absolute is the fertile womb giving forth every possibility and every permutation of blissful being. This is the great blessing of impermanence. You are all of it, all that ever was and ever shall be, world without end. Amen.

Namaste,
Shunyamurti

About the Author

Shunyamurti is the founder and research director of the Sat Yoga Institute, headquartered in Costa Rica. The institute's mission is to accelerate the transformation of human consciousness and contribute to the spiritual and cultural renaissance that is fermenting now on our planet. Shunyamurti was inspired to lead such an effort as a result of his own inner work that has led to attunement with the ultimate source of consciousness.

Shunyamurti's spiritual path has been wide-ranging and profound. It has included many years of Yogic training, in diverse forms of Yoga, including five years of intensive practice of classical Ashtanga Yoga followed by ten years spent in a formal Raja Yoga monastic order, and many more years of meditative practice in diverse spiritual traditions. He has also deeply studied numerous other transformational disciplines, from shamanism to various schools of psychology and psychoanalysis.

His spiritual experiences began early, with an interest in poetry writing. The practice of searching inwardly to discover words to express his innermost sense of being led him to a serendipitous auto-initiation in the practice of meditation. Soon, the interest in actual poems was replaced with a fascination with the fount of intelligence and feeling itself. This culminated in a mystical realization of the presence of God.

A more systematic study of religion followed. He worked with a teacher of Kabbalah and learned other ways of entering into contemplative prayer. He was later influenced by esoteric Christian and Sufi approaches to God-consciousness. He lived attuned to the Divine Presence. After entering college, he was faced with the problem of how to respond to the military draft, and his conscience would not permit him to support the use of violence. He discovered the writings of Gandhi and began a deep and long-lasting study of the roots of aggression in the human soul, beginning with himself. In addition to taking the Yogic vow of *ahimsa*, he studied many ways of transforming destructive energy into creative power. This led to the practice of various martial arts for many years, including judo and aikido, kung fu and tai chi, as meditative means of channeling aggressive energies into a force of peace. This also led him to the study of Zen, and later of other forms of Buddhist and Taoist thought and practice.

During that period, Shunyamurti also experimented with entheogens, discovering both the power and the limits of botanical and chemical substances in opening the doors of perception. He studied with shamanic teachers many native ways of gaining the alliance of the powers of nature and entering into paranormal states for healing, communion with higher beings, and deepening ecstatic wisdom. He experimented with fasting, and discovered another portal to the infinite that opened on long fasts of forty days and more, and he came to understand the internal biological component of the production of *soma*, the divine nectar of bliss, in the human brain.

All of this informal spiritual education added dimensions of understanding to what he was learning in his formal education, which focused on the fields of philosophy, theater, and political science. Eventually, he also earned a degree in law. But his spiritual calling led him on a vision quest that resulted in a decisive out-of-body experience, an ascension that determined his life course away from the professional practice of law and fully into the life of a yogi and mystic, and further training toward becoming a spiritual guide.

Led by the higher power to an ashram in India, he entered into constant practice of the remembrance of God. As a consequence, ever more extraordinary and more ego-shattering encounters with the Absolute ensued. In the ashram, he was often asked for help and counsel, and in deep dialogue with his fellow yogis, he came to understand what he still needed to learn to unravel their karmic knots and thus fulfill his own destiny. He returned to the U.S. to study hypnotherapy, after which he opened a private practice. At the same time, he pursued a doctoral program in psychology, and began a rigorous study of Jungian analysis and other forms of transpersonal theory. His meditative practice continued to deepen, rapturous uprushes of kundalini occurred often, ecstatic moments unfolded in which time would stop and the miraculous fact of eternity manifested. Consciousness became continually more saturated with the realization of nonduality.

Shunyamurti also became an ever more serious student of dreamwork and symptomatology, which led to the study of Freudian psychoanalysis, especially in its Lacanian and other postmodern approaches. This opened out into a deeper study of Western philosophy—from the Pythagoreans and pre-Socratics to the neo-platonists of ancient Greece to medieval thinkers including Nicolas of Cusa, Thomas Aquinas, Meister Eckhart, and others, including in the field of alchemy, to the founders of modern thought, including Descartes, Spinoza, Hegel, and Schelling, to the contemporary theorists of phenomenology, hermeneutics, deconstruction, and post-structuralism.

He studied logic, language, semiotics, and sciences such as quantum physics, which gave him more nuanced symbolic concepts with which to understand his own immersion in super-consciousness. He was able to synthesize his realization of Advaita, the ultimate truth of nonduality, with the fragmented and elided nature of ego-consciousness, and thus to be able to guide others to complete the purification of the unconscious, and traverse its phantasms to realize the Oneness beyond the event horizon of the ego.

The absolute emptiness of transfinite potentiality, called by Spinoza *Natura Naturans*, became palpably reunited with the forms of the phenomenal plane, *Natura Naturata*. Shunyamurti recognized this as the original intention of Yoga practice, and reconstituted

Yoga on a conceptual foundation that would be more coherent to the modern Western mind. He further refined this approach, which came to be called Sat Yoga (meaning union with the Ground of Being), and he became increasingly adept as a healer and teacher, and a remover of obstacles for those on the spiritual path. A large and unique corpus of higher knowledge was accumulating, ready to be disseminated for the benefit of other seekers.

Before moving to Costa Rica, Shunyamurti maintained his flourishing private practice as a transformational healer in California for over twenty years, integrating the healing effects of unitive presence with such modalities as hypnotherapy, psychoanalysis, family systems approaches, gestalt, transpersonal and Jungian work, in addition to several forms of bodywork and kundalini energy transmission. He connects always with the resonant presence of Ramana Maharshi and Nisargadatta Maharaj as his closest teachers, for whom he feels the deepest reverence.

In 2001, Shunyamurti received another vision, to build an "ark" to survive the cataclysms of a world in chaos. SYI was designed to be an advanced spiritual school and ultimately a self-sustaining creative eco-community that could serve as a transitional medium to bring humans from the present state of ego-consciousness to the next state, that of full Self-realization and reintegration with the Cosmic Intelligence. He foresaw that Costa Rica would become a major center of the new global culture of peace. Thus was the Sat Yoga Institute conceived.

Shunyamurti functions now as a spiritual guide, retreat leader, and teacher, and he is engaged in spiritual community building, in addition to his ongoing advanced research in the Yogic sciences. He can be reached through the Institute's website: www.Satyogainstitute.org. The Sat Yoga Institute offers ongoing psycho-spiritual training and accepts sincere volunteers who seek the opportunity to enter into an intensive process of Self-realization.